Mornings With My Cat Mii

Mornings With My Cat Mii

MAYUMI INABA

Translated from the Japanese by
Ginny Tapley Takemori

Harvill *Secker*

LONDON

5 7 9 10 8 6

Harvill Secker, an imprint of Vintage, is part of the Penguin Random
House group of companies whose addresses can be found at
global.penguinrandomhouse.com

First published by Harvill Secker in 2024
First published in Japanese with the title ミーのいない朝 / *Mii No Inai Asa*
in 1999 by Kawade Shobo Shinsha Ltd. Publishers, Tokyo
This English edition arranged with Kawade Shobo Shinsha Ltd. Publishers
through The English Agency (Japan) Ltd. And New River Literary Ltd.

Copyright © Yuji Hirano 1999
English translation copyright © Ginny Tapley Takamori 2024

penguin.co.uk/vintage

Typeset in 11.5/15.6pt Calluna by Jouve (UK), Milton Keynes
Printed and bound in Great Britain by Clays Ltd, Elcograf S.p.A.

The authorised representative in the EEA is Penguin Random House Ireland,
Morrison Chambers, 32 Nassau Street, Dublin D02 YH68

A CIP catalogue record for this book is available from the British Library

ISBN 9781787304413

Penguin Random House is committed to a sustainable future
for our business, our readers and our planet. This book is made
from Forest Stewardship Council® certified paper.

Contents

CONTENTS

I

A Kitten on the Breeze

Our First Place

It was the end of summer, 1977. At least I think it was late summer. I found a cat, a little ball of fluff. A teeny tiny baby kitten.

Her face was the size of a coin, and was split by her huge wide-open mouth as she hung suspended in the dark. She was stuck in the fence of a junior high school on the banks of the Tamagawa River in the Y neighbour-hood of Fuchu City in western Tokyo.

What direction was the wind blowing that night? It was most likely a gentle breeze blowing up to my house from the river. I followed her cries as they carried on this breeze. At first I searched the gaps in the hedge around my house and in among the weeds of the empty plots on my street. But her cries were coming from high up, not low down. I looked up and suddenly saw a little white dot.

The large expanse of the school grounds was shrouded in the dim light. Before me was a high fence separating the road and the school. Somebody must have shoved the kitten into the fence. She was hanging so high up that even on tiptoe, I could barely reach her as she clung on for dear life.

With sharp pointy ears, innocent glistening eyes and a pink slit of a mouth, she was puffing her body up as much as she could to stop herself from falling, looking down at me fearfully. It was obvious that she hadn't dropped there out of nowhere or climbed up by herself, but had been put there deliberately out of malice or mischief.

'Come with me . . .'

I reached out my arms and the tiny kitten clung on to me with surprising strength. She was freezing cold, a helpless little thing. I hugged her to my chest and a sweet animal scent filled my nostrils. Her body was infused with the smell of milk and summer. The smooth feel of soft baby fur filled the palm of my hand.

She couldn't have been long born, yet she already had perfectly formed needle-sharp claws, and her nose and mouth and everything about her was tiny and adorable. As I stroked her, she leaned her entire body weight into me, helplessly light, and bumped her head against me a few times.

I didn't know where her mother was, or whether she had been dumped or had strayed from her mother and got lost before someone put her into the fence. All I knew was that she must have felt utterly desperate hanging up there, and I just wanted to give her somewhere cosy to rest at least for the night. Did I have any milk at home?

I'd have to find a box where she could feel safe . . . My mind full of such thoughts, I hugged her to my chest and rushed back home.

'A kitten,' I told my husband as I ran into the kitchen. 'She was crying outside.' I held her up by the scruff of her neck for him to see. 'Look how little she is!' My cotton shirt made a ripping sound as I peeled her away from my chest. In the light I could see she had a pretty face. She was a calico, with white, black and tan stripes on her head and patches on her back, and a belly that was pure white.

It was over twenty years ago now, but I can still clearly remember that tiny kitten's sharp claws. I'll never forget how she innocently butted her little head against my chest, either. Or the breeze that night. Those cries from the school fence would never have reached me without it. Maybe it delivered her cries to my window. Perhaps by some ghostly chance the breeze from the river had a magical power that night.

The breeze came in waves from the river up to the houses in my neighbourhood. Maybe it was the quality of the water, but to me it always seemed to have a refreshing smell of liquor, and it was so pleasant, neither too strong nor too cold, that in summer and autumn I wanted to keep my windows open all the time. Or maybe it was thanks to the power of my windows that I found my cat.

Three years or so after we moved to Tokyo, I abruptly

stopped making yellow curtains. In the little house we'd lived in before this one, I'd been obsessed with making yellow curtains and yellow cushions.

Our first house had been on the banks of the Edogawa in eastern Tokyo. It was a new residential development in which all the houses were two storeys, all the same shape with the same layout of rooms, all tightly packed together. The land had been carved up and sold off, with houses crammed in as tightly as possible with no space at all for anything like gardens, and so close together that if you put your ear against the wall you could hear the sound of the TV or voices next door.

Within a month of moving in, I realised the house was full of dust mixed with yellow sand. The sand relentlessly got into the cracks between the tatami mats, and in the rails of the sash window frames, and it turned my duster yellow in no time at all. After battling for weeks against this yellow dust brought on the breeze from goodness knows where, to counter it I finally decided to furnish the house with rugs made from yellow and orange fabrics, yellow curtains, and yellow and lemon-coloured cushions. If I covered everything in the same colour, the dust wouldn't be so visible any more. As a result, our house was filled to the rafters with pop colours and just stepping inside it felt like being in a meadow of poppies. Yet even such desperate measures didn't solve the problem of the yellow sand.

I was only cured of this yellow sickness when we

moved out west to Fuchu City. We were still living near a river here, but the breeze was completely different.

We had come to this house on the banks of the Tamagawa in the spring of 1975. It belonged to my husband's colleague A, who had been transferred by their company to another part of the country and had rented it to us so we could keep an eye on it. It was a comfortable house with a child's swing in the garden. It had a spacious south-facing living room separated from a bright kitchen by a counter, in addition to two Japanese-style rooms and a small storeroom.

All the rooms had windows with a good view outside. There was plenty of space between us and the surrounding houses, and you couldn't hear any noise through the walls.

Houses are strange. Inside they have voices, a sense of presence. Rooms have their own smell, but also air that is embracing and tender. Maybe the heart of the person who built a house permeates its every corner. Even though this house in Fuchu belonged to someone else, unlike our previous place it always had a pleasant aspect.

I stopped buying yellow fabrics. White suited our new place. The curtains were white, and the house looked prettiest with minimal furnishings. I didn't place any rugs on the floor. The sensation of bare feet on the wooden floors became the essence of home.

I grew accustomed to the sight of the swing swaying in the breeze and to the soft, warm touch of the grass in the garden. Even though the sofa and most of the tableware and other contents of the kitchen cupboards belonged to someone else, after six months I already felt as though we'd been living there for years. I loved strolling along the river embankment at dusk on my days off, gazing at the surface of the water.

In early spring dogwood bloomed white and pink outside the houses, and wooded areas here and there were full of the white flowers of robinia trees. We'd moved into this house in spring but, before we knew it, it was already autumn and the landscape was changing rapidly.

I only realised that the trees in front of our house were robinias when the white flowers came into bloom. When I opened the windows, the curtains puffed up in the breeze carrying their dense fragrance. The blossoms made the whole neighbourhood feel cheerful. I had never lived anywhere with such a fragrant breeze before.

My days were now so peaceful I could scarcely believe I had once been possessed by the yellow sickness.

It was at this point that I met my cat. She would never have been able to sneak into my lightened heart the way she did had this place not been colourless and transparent. I was giddily happy, no longer irritated by the sand or continually running around with a duster. Maybe it was because my defences were down that I readily welcomed her into my life after our eyes met, our skin came into contact, and I set off walking without a second thought.

8

Kitten   tiny
Claws   see-through   like egg white
Ears   moving   listening
Eyes   moist   limpid
The faint smell of liquor in the neighbourhood
       night
You've come from far away
Welcome   hello
Me human   you cat

Another Cat I Remember

Had I always liked cats?

The only cat I'd ever known was the one we'd had at our home in the Nagoya countryside in the late 1950s. That cat had belonged to an old lady called Tsune who lived with us, but he'd often go missing and the whole family would be in uproar trying to find him.

His name had been Shiro. Whenever I recalled Shiro, what came to mind was a plump white cat walking clumsily over all the futons airing in the veranda and on the roof. That was Shiro. He had been in our home for as long as I could remember and I didn't know where he had come from or how he'd come there. When I asked my mother she just tilted her head questioningly and said she vaguely remembered someone having given him to Tsune.

Tsune was my mother's aunt. She had married twice but both marriages had ended unhappily and she'd come back home, and was already living with my family by the time I was born. Her first marriage had ended when she couldn't have children and was sent home, and the second after her husband became involved with another woman. Both of those misfortunes were due to the male chauvinism of a feudalistic household system, and both had made her a somewhat difficult woman.

Her disposition was a mix of hysteria and depression that constantly created waves in the house. My father, who had been adopted into the family as the heir, disliked dealing with her and kept well out of her way, while Tsune herself had no doubt had her fill of men.

The only presence in the house that she had any affection for at all was her cat Shiro, and as long as Shiro was with her she would be in a good mood. Upon closer observation, she was an ambivalent mix of childishness and intransigence, either of which would hold sway depending on her mood in the moment.

It was when Shiro disappeared that Tsune grew hysterical, and she would run around searching for him, calling his name. She wasn't alone. Searching with her was Shiiko, a woman with no relatives of her own who had settled herself in the house as a kind of companion to Tsune long before I was born.

Tsune was childless and Shiiko had no family. In some ways they were similar, but what was interesting about their friendship was the way that Shiiko blindly obeyed Tsune. Shiiko was said to have suffered a brain disease as a child, and she didn't know her own mother's name or remember anything about the house she had grown up in.

Her childhood memories seemed particularly vague, and whenever anyone asked her about her mother or family, she would always answer, 'I don't know. I just don't know.' If anyone pushed her further on the matter, she stopped talking and got so flustered she would start crying.

Shiiko often looked after me when I was little, and in my child's mind I always wondered what it would have been like not to have parents or not to know where you'd been born, and felt sad.

Shiiko was the one who took care of Shiro. After meals she would put the leftovers in his bowl, go around wiping his muddy pawprints with a cloth, and when he disappeared she would spend much of the day looking for him. This hunt for Shiro was a daily occurrence, and the sight of Shiiko running around was a sign that she had been infected by Tsune's search for her cat.

Calling 'Shiro's gone missing. Shiro! Shiro!', Shiiko would first rush to the chicken coop that Shiro liked so much, then into the garden, and from the garden she would go through the main gate, peek in the storehouse, then go out into the fields and the bamboo grove.

I didn't know if this was typical behaviour for cats or whether it was just Shiro, but he was always going missing. Thinking about him now, I wonder whether he used to visit the neighbours, or whether he had a favourite spot in the fields where he would go to play, but he seemed to spend more time outside than at home. And

Shiiko was constantly running around after him. She knew very well that Tsune would be in a good mood whenever Shiro was home, and so she couldn't help going out to look for him.

'Is Shiro around?' Tsune would ask Shiiko. If he was, she would answer, 'Yes, he is,' but if he wasn't she would be out like a shot searching for him. The way she ran off was so frantic that my mother and I couldn't help laughing. 'Shiiko's looking for the cat again!' we'd say. This was all very well, but sometimes both Shiiko and the cat would still be missing when we needed help getting dinner ready or with neighbourhood duties.

Amid all the uproar my father would pull a face as though he'd swallowed a fly and mutter, 'That damned cat again.'

When we started hearing shrill conversations around the house – 'Is Shiro there?' 'No, he's not!' 'No? But he was here at lunchtime. We'll have to keep looking. What *are* you doing?' – the whole house would be on tenterhooks, knowing that Tsune was getting hysterical.

'I don't suppose it could be one of those shamisen makers, could it?' she would screech. 'Shiiko, have you checked in the wells?'

At that time, you would often get tradesmen specialising in catching cats in the countryside to use their skin on shamisen. They would deftly garotte the cat with a tool made of thin rolled wire. Also, there were two wells on our property. Tsune's fears always ended up in the same conclusions: either Shiro had been caught by a cat killer or he had fallen into a well.

But when Shiro was sleeping on the veranda or in the garden, Tsune would look utterly at peace. On cold winter days, as the coals glowed red in the brazier, Shiro would be curled up asleep next to it with Tsune huddled up absently warming her hands over it. At times like these, with nothing in particular to do, Shiiko would sit in the corner of the room smiling. Even when Shiro walked over the futons with muddy paws, Tsune would just laugh, 'Oh no, Shiro . . . !' My mother was always the one to clean Shiro's muddy pawprints off the futons, but she would just say, 'Shiro again!', as though she was used to it. Sometimes, if she hadn't had time to do it or just couldn't be bothered, his pawprints were clearly visible at nose level on the children's futons laid out at bedtime.

Entirely unconcerned by the commotion and laments of the adults, Shiro would continue to abscond regularly. Searching for him in the wide-open fields and bamboo groves of the countryside was no easy matter. My mother would always laugh in amusement at Shiiko running around in her worn-out geta calling, 'Shiro! Shiro!', her voice getting progressively thinner until finally it sounded as worn as an overstretched rubber band.

'She might as well give up. But I suppose it takes her mind off it too.'

Shiiko herself probably got fed up with Tsune always wanting her around.

Whenever Tsune went out, Shiiko would accompany her. She would traipse after her carrying her bundle and kicking the hem of her short kimono so that it flapped about. She would probably have preferred to relax at home while Tsune was out but could never say so to her face, so searching for Shiro was her chance to taste a bit of freedom away from her.

There were all sorts of plants growing on the paths through the fields, and while Shiiko was searching for Shiro she would pluck fruit from a large fig tree and put it in her mouth. On the banks of the river behind the house she would watch flies, crucian carps and crayfish flitting around in the river while pretending to look for Shiro. Sometimes she would squat down amid all the cosmos and chrysanthemums blooming in the back garden. 'Shiiko, what are you doing?' I once asked her. 'I'm looking for Shiro,' she answered. So I crouched down with her beneath the cosmos flowers pretending to look for Shiro. 'Copycat!' I said, and did a pee.

Even now, all these decades later, the sound of Tsune's shrill voice calling night and day for Shiro still echoes in my ears, but I've come to understand that lacking a family and children of her own, Shiro was the only one she could relate to.

I have absolutely no recollection of how or when Shiro disappeared from the house or how he died, but from time to time Tsune's distant voice would reach me on the wind, making me feel strangely desolate and melancholy.

Looking at old photographs, Tsune always had the corners of her mouth set in a grimace. Not having known happiness as a woman, instead having fallen victim to men and societal norms, had given her a fierce gaze and strong jawline. There was even something of a big cat glaring out of the shadows about her. Her eyes appeared to be rejecting something, to be repressing some inexpressible emotion. The eyes of a woman that had entirely left behind any softness, that were dignified but also somewhat unapproachable.

In contrast, when Shiro was with her, her face seemed to melt. Tsune and Shiro basking in the sun on the veranda, Tsune and Shiro beside the large brazier with a heat shimmer rising from it. Tsune and Shiro together, luxuriating in the heat from the sun and the fire.

As a child, life went on whether Shiro was there or not. When he was at home, I naturally accepted his presence and would play with him, and when he wasn't around I naturally accepted the fact there was going to be a big fuss again. Only my father was irritated by him.

My father often used to say things like, 'Cats are such creepy creatures, noiselessly rubbing up against your legs like that.' He also said they were duplicitous animals. 'You never know what they're thinking!' Dogs were different. According to him, even if you kept dogs on a leash all day, they knew that was their place. He was a dog person, through and through.

Oblivious to what was said of him, Shiro would nap

on the veranda without a care in the world and roam as he liked, paying no heed to the hysterical exchanges between Tsune and Shiiko.

And the same commotion would happen every day, with Tsune wailing that Shiro had disappeared, and Shiiko dashing off around the garden and fields at dusk. Watching all this going on, with no understanding of the nature of these animals, I couldn't help but wonder at the humans running around and having their days disrupted all because of a cat.

My Cat's Name

The kitten I'd brought in from the dark was completely different from the Shiro of my memories. This little newborn bundle did not know how to hide, and pushed her face into my hand seeking milk, searching between my fingers, tottering helplessly around. My husband and I took the milk from the refrigerator and poured some into a dish, gathered some old towels, and sat nervously watching her.

I was shocked at the sheer number of fleas on her. I hadn't noticed when I found her, but now in the light I could see her belly, her back, her tail were crawling with so many fleas that I had to wonder where they had all come from.

Meanwhile, the tiny kitten plunged bodily into the rags on the kitchen table as though having a seizure, trying to get to the milk. Every time we brought our faces close to the dish of milk, though, she looked up warily with innocent eyes. She couldn't have been long in this world, so how come she had already learned the vigilance of feral cats? It was heartrending to see. Maybe her mother had been fearful of humans. Or maybe she had naturally learned to fear people after having been abandoned. When she looked up at me with her beautiful clear eyes, I saw something like an animal instinct she had acquired from birth flit across them.

But however wary she was, however much she looked up at me like that, what made me realise that she must have been suddenly taken away from her mother's milk was the way she still couldn't use her tongue properly. Even when she tried to lap up the milk, she immediately started choking on it. Seeing her stick her face in the milk and start choking, mewling pathetically, I felt helpless. How could we get her to drink?

We were totally overwhelmed with all the fleas on the kitten's body. However many we removed, she was still teeming with fat glossy fleas all over, behind her ears, on her back, in the hollow of her belly. Did animals always carry so many parasites from birth? Every time we parted some fur, we would see one of the nimble black things burying back into it.

My husband and I kept turning over the kitten's tiny body, spreading her legs, moving her mercilessly this way and that searching for fleas. 'There's one!' we would exclaim. 'There goes another!' The fleas we crushed between our nails floated on the surface of the water in the washbasin like sesame seeds. As soon as we'd decided that was enough for today, yet more would appear, and however many we removed, they didn't seem to diminish in number at all.

It took us days to come up with a name for her. Naming an animal is hard, really hard. I would come up with names like Ringo, Umi, Muru, Tama, but end up crying, 'Oh, I just don't know!' However hard I thought, I just couldn't think of a name that suited this little kitten. My husband said flippantly that it didn't matter if she didn't have a name, but it was so inconvenient. How was I supposed to call her without a name? And it occurred to me that the only real difference between stray cats and pet cats was whether or not they had a name.

Meanwhile, we were calling her 'she' or 'the little one'. Then one day, we started calling her Mimi. The kitten cried an astonishing amount, whenever she wanted milk or played with the curtains or struggled while we were removing fleas. Her high-pitched *mii-mii* sounded somehow sad, as though she was calling for her mother, and made my chest constrict. This *mii-mii* got short-ened to Mimi, but the name didn't last long. It proved somewhat tricky to say Mimi out loud, and my tongue stumbled over it every time.

After a few days, then, Mimi got shortened even further to just Mii.

Later, I would sigh over the fancy names people gave to their cats: Randy, Jajamaru, Sasuke, Marilyn, and so on. All of my friends' cats and the numerous cats in books I browsed at the bookshop, or the cats that I came across in novels or newspaper columns – all of them had names with an appropriately cute ring to them.

My cat was called simply Mii. We sometimes nick-named her Mii-tan, but her formal name was Mii Inaba. I simply couldn't manage to come up with a better name for her, however hard I tried. Her *mew-mii, mew-mii* way of crying that I'd first heard when she was hanging there in the dark had somehow stuck in my heart and wouldn't go away.

And thereafter, whenever I called her name, she would naturally answer me, *mii*. Mii had decided on her own name with the sound of her cries.

> *Nobody knows   your real name*
> *From a dark corner in our new neighbourhood*
> *You were a voice that came raining down*
> *Like stars   like gems*
> *Like little grains of light   knock-knocking on*
>   *the door*
> *Music was playing in the distance   maybe Yesterday*
> *Your yesterday   singing*
> *Telling of the past saying goodbye to today*
>   *singing in the distance*
> *I wanted to believe it*
> *Like a freshly laid egg   a brand-new you*
> *Maybe I should have called you Tomorrow*
> *Or maybe Dawn*
>
> *Where do names come from?*
> *You answer simply, mii*

Under the Robinia Blossoms

Back then I was working for a small interior design company in Shinjuku. Every day I would draw up plans, visit client worksites, attend meetings, and only get home around nine o'clock at night. Upon reaching Fuchu, I would be propelled out of the train on the wave of people and change on to a local train. The second stop was Nakagawara, the closest station to my home. As I came out of the ticket gate, I would walk briskly along streets of flowering dogwood lit up by streetlights and paths dotted with trees. The moment I got home, the first thing I did was search for Mii and greet her, 'Tadaima!' Her development as the seasons passed became the main topic of conversation between me and my husband.

Since Mii came into our life, the range of items on my shopping list and the type of stores I frequented had suddenly expanded. Until then I'd never so much as set foot inside a pet shop, but now when I went into town I naturally gravitated to them, and would head up to browse the rooftop outlets of department stores in places like Shinjuku and Ginza.

And I would always make some discovery or other there. There weren't as many products available as there are today, but still there were various types of canned wet food and dry food in boxes or bags. My gaze wandered here and there, and I would end up picking things up to look at them even if I had no intention of buying them, astonished at the sheer variety, with flavours like horse mackerel, bonito and chicken.

Mii was still mainly dependent on milk, and needed things to play with more than anything else, so I bought her lots of toys, selecting whatever I thought she might enjoy every time payday came around. One was a cute ball made of woven bamboo with a bell inside it. There were also toys in the shape of mice and rabbits. Toys that were round and good for rolling, just the right size for a kitten's tiny paws. Some were lifelike, others were cheap-looking soft rubber ones. So many toys!

Once I discovered that she liked solid objects with a string attached, I found myself making all kinds of toys for her, attaching things like a broken brooch to the end of a piece of wool, or adding the little bells from a key holder, and later on using buttons or pencil stubs. I would call, 'Hey, Mii,' and throw these home-made playthings, and she would jump at them and tirelessly chase them around, so the floor ended up strewn in objects with trailing strings.

Mii's favourite was a sewing machine bobbin wound with whatever thread or wool I had to hand. It lurched along erratically when I rolled it across the floor, and these unpredictable movements attracted her interest. She would bat it with her paw and jump back, then bat it again and watch it wobbling along with a surprised look on her face.

Early on, the most useful things I bought were the syringes and baby bottle I got from the pharmacy. Mii still wasn't able to drink milk out of a saucer. At first I tried feeding her milk through a straw, but if I wasn't careful her mouth would fill with liquid and she would choke. Then I tried a syringe, but Mii quickly learned to drink from a baby bottle.

Seeing this tiny kitten lying on the kitchen table hugging a bottle bigger than herself to her belly as she suckled milk always made me smile. It must have felt very different from her mother's belly and nipples, but just the smell of milk seemed to give her the will to survive and she suckled on it ferociously. She was so happy her voice became shrill with a strangely hoarse *fugya, fugya* that I only ever heard when she was suckling. She looked just like a sea otter with food placed on its belly.

I spent all my days off occupied with Mii. I would watch her squatting on the toilet as she learned to pee on the kitty litter I'd bought at the pet shop, and I would crouch down on the floor to gaze at her noisily lapping up her milk. On days where there was no breeze, I would deliberately shake the curtains so she could play with them all day long.

When she started timidly venturing out into the garden, we made new games, with me rolling her around on the grass, and sitting with her in a sunny spot on the terrace, removing fleas from her fur. This had became part of the daily routine, and I discovered the most effective method was a stainless-steel comb with tightly spaced teeth that the pet shop had recommended. A lot of fur came out when I combed her with it. The fleas were in among that fur, and there were a staggering number of them.

More! And yet more! Five . . . seven . . . twelve . . . twenty fleas! Gleefully I submerged the comb full of fleas in a bucket of washing-up liquid, taking cruel pleasure in watching them die.

Mii was always there when I came home from work. She was getting bigger by the day and started wanting to go out at all times of the day and night. The garden quickly became part of her territory, and she also took a liking to the little copse of robinia trees opposite our house. She would rub her body on the ground, smelling the grass.

I still remember those robinias in the first spring after Mii came to us. The blossoms that rained down profusely from the tops of the sparse, skinny trees. The beautiful contrast between the blue sky and white flowers, and the sweet fragrance that emanated from them. How both Mii and I loved those trees! Every morning I would open the windows and breathe in a deep lungful of their scent. When there was a breeze, even the fragrance trembled and I would be filled with a languidness that made me feel sleepy. The blossoms piled up, turning the ground soft and white. Walking over them, the cool sensation of the flowers was transmitted to my feet through the soles of my shoes.

Mii stepped gingerly over them, sniffing them intently.

But her territory was still limited, and she never went very far or anywhere she didn't know. She was appallingly timid. She would walk apprehensively over the lawn in the garden. And when she ventured out to the robinias, she proceeded cautiously, continually turning to look at me. If someone she didn't know happened to pass by, she would flatten her ears and come rushing back, and at the sound of a car she would freeze on the spot.

She was so nervous and alert to everything in the outside world that I had to wonder if she really was a cat. Maybe she was a new type of animal, a coward with the face of a cat!

I soon realised something: this kitten was scared of heights. It didn't matter who was holding her, the moment she looked down she would start shaking. The memory of having been suspended from a hole in the fence soon after she was born must have been per-manently engraved into her little brain. She could be purring loudly, but the moment I picked her up her purrs faded and I could feel her start trembling in my arms and I would hurriedly put her back down on the floor. It took Mii a long time to get used to heights.

I also noticed a rather strange habit of hers. Whenever she sat on something fluffy, like a woollen sweater or a soft rug, she would start kneading with her front paws. This must have been a throwback to when she kneaded her mother for milk, and these soft items seemed to trigger the memory. Even now, after having been separated from her mother, her body had retained this instinctual nursing behaviour.

These two observations led me to revise all the knowledge I had gleaned from reading numerous books on cats.

For example, I had one book that was a splendid photography collection. One of the many chapters was on cat biology, where it was stated that cats' memories were erased after a few minutes.

Later on I heard about cats that had been dumped far from home, only to find their way back several months later. How they remembered landscapes and smells wasn't known, but there must be a part of an animal's anatomy responsible for memory. Ever since Mii had been separated from the ground and left hanging in space, fear and terror had been seared into her memory just as they were in humans. She always opened her pink mouth wide and screamed, 'I don't like heights!'

My image of Mii was inextricably imbued with the cool breeze of our neighbourhood in Fuchu, and the colour and fragrance of robinia blossoms. Wherever I was, just calling her name evoked the breeze blowing up from the river and the fragrance of the blossoms, and these had come to symbolise where Mii had come from.

Mii never tired of gazing at these white objects dropping from somewhere high up above her, and every time a flower landed on her nose she flinched and, losing her balance, toppled over. I could watch this for ever, and when the blossoms ended and everything turned green I felt somehow disappointed, 'See you again next year,' I would say – not for Mii's sake, but for my own.

Fun   in colours   in smells
Beneath the trees   peach   quince   robinia
Playing   playing   caressed by the breeze
This is spring!   At least for humans
But   you don't know spring
You just enjoy   the fragrant breeze
Full of curiosity   watching

Counting on my fingers   one day   another day
Will the blossoms fall today   or tomorrow?
Divining fingers and moving petals
Mii   these are fingers   these are flowers
My cat playing   fingers   flowers
*   in the enigma of spring*

2

A Premonition of Parting

Moving House

But Mii did not get to enjoy the fragrance of the robinia the following year.

At the end of September 1978, we had to move again. A was transferred back to Tokyo, and we needed to vacate his house. We had been living in Fuchu for three years.

Thinking back to our life then, I recall how very busy my husband and I both were. I have no idea how we managed to find time to search for another house. He was often away on business, and he never knew when he might be transferred to another location for work, just as A had been. We had originally lived in the suburbs of Nagoya, and had moved to Tokyo when his company had suddenly transferred him. He could be transferred again at any time.

Those days were strangely unsettling, maybe due to the nature of the city of Tokyo or maybe of society as a whole. The mechanical blip-bleep sounds of the Space Invader game echoed around arcades, and the Pink Lady pop song 'UFO' ('If we just held hands and gazed at each other . . .') was playing wherever you went. At the same time there were many scary news reports about the increasing numbers of people committing suicide or disappearing due to loan sharks, and rumours abounded of the kuchisake onna, a yokai resembling a woman with a wide slit-open mouth.

Japan was emerging from the post-war poverty and it wasn't so clear whether society was rich or poor or just in high spirits. My husband was insanely busy. He worked for a foreign company that manufactured things like paper cups, paper napkins and the paper tape used in ikebana flower arrangements, right at a time when there was a busy food service industry and lots of flower-arranging classes in cultural centres, so demand for their products was increasing and business was thriving. With his packed schedule of entertaining clients, attending meetings and socialising until late with colleagues and superiors, it was nigh-on impossible for him to go around estate agents, and so the search for a new house fell to me.

At the time we were barely making ends meet, despite both of us working. There was no question of having enough savings to buy a house, and we couldn't hope to find anywhere within easy commuting distance of central Tokyo. On top of that we now had Mii. We would somehow get by with just the two of us, but when it came to renting somewhere that allowed pets, Tokyo could only be described as problematic. Wherever I went I was met with rejection, mostly on some vague or unclear pretext. It seemed the mere mention of a dog or cat evoked some kind of nuisance or trouble for the neighbourhood, or maybe there really were many such cases, for the estate agent's response would be simply, 'A cat? Ah, that's tricky,' or even a blunt, 'No rentals for pets.'

Still, I had to find something. Somewhere as convenient as possible for commuting, ideally a detached house (I really hoped we could get a house, even an old one, with a garden for Mii), with a cheap rent and, on top of that, a willingness to accept pets. There were some properties that met the first three conditions, but none of them would tolerate a cat.

I lost track of how much time I spent going around countless estate agents. In the end, though, I got lucky. While my search for a house was proving absurdly difficult and unproductive, I was browsing the property file at the umpteenth estate agent I'd visited and I suddenly noticed a house in Kokubunji, just north of where we currently lived. It was like a ray of light! For the first time I realised that some available properties were not included in ads or estate agent listings in magazines. The catch was that it was only available as a short-term let.

The house looked like it had been tailor-made for us to live together with Mii. It was a shabby old one-storey wooden house with a south-facing veranda. Opposite was a shrine surrounded by a little cedar forest, and what's more the bare earth of its spacious precincts had not been asphalted over. The house had a small garden with a sandpit, and had been planted with a peach tree as well as quince, sacred lily and kerria. The border with the shrine grounds was marked by a fairly high concrete-block wall.

The Koigakubo district, two stops along the Musashino Line from Kokubunji, had apparently long been popular with horticulturalists, and trees grew abundant and lush in the area. The house was surrounded by fields of soil that was black, sticky and glossy, and the neighbourhood was quiet and secluded. A soft smell of water hung in the air, possibly from the local spring.

'What do you think?'

The estate agent walked around opening windows. With each one, I felt more than just light shining into my heart. The windows faced south and I could see the green cedars of the shrine and gingko trees near by. The Japanese-style construction had a corridor encircling the north side. The rooms were in an old-fashioned layout, with an 8-mat living room with a tokonoma alcove and an adjacent 6-mat tatami room, and another 4.5-mat tatami room jutting out southwards forming an L-shape. Separated from them, at the end of the corridor on the north side, was a wooden-floored kitchen.

The initial rent was only 50,000 yen. This was way below the market price as the house came with the condition that the contract would only be for the two years' duration of the owner's job transfer.

Managing the property were Mr and Mrs T, the owner's elderly parents, who lived in a house with an iron gate on the adjoining plot of land. Our house was incon-spicuously hidden away behind theirs, and surrounded by a concrete-block wall. What's more, it was in a cul-de-sac at the end of the lane.

Oh, what a lovely house it was! I could have danced for joy. The house was quite old and could never be described as sunny, shaded as it was by the trees of the shrine. But I doubted I could ever describe a house as lovely, however stylish it might be, unless I thought Mii would be happy there.

I had found a house where we could live with Mii. That was all that mattered.

But I must confess that I never could bring myself to tell Mr and Mrs T that we had a cat. Whenever I'd men-tioned her to an estate agent, things had always ended badly. I couldn't bear the thought of this house falling through too. I really didn't want to lose it. After we moved in, I would hold my breath whenever Mii miaowed and listen for any reaction from the house next door. I just hoped that Mr and Mrs T somehow wouldn't notice . . .

In the end they never did mention anything about a cat, or reproach me. I still don't know whether they really didn't notice her or whether they just turned a blind eye, but I feel there must have been some kind of tacit permission.

There were many great things about that house other than our tolerant neighbours that made it so wonderful.

The best gift was that there were good gaps that

35

allowed Mii to come and go. The lean-to attached to the bathroom provided Mii with a way in and out of the house. It was small, just big enough to hold some old timber and rusty shovels and the like, but its corrugated-plastic walls were slightly torn. Mii was able to squeeze through the hole to go out to the shrine grounds and play beneath the ginkgo trees.

The cedars in the shrine grounds also provided welcome shade for the whole house. The tatami mats and paper fusuma doors were all new, but it was the sort of house where you knew right away that the fresh green tatami would absorb the light, gradually fade to amber, and become smooth and familiar to the touch. The pillars had taken on a rich colour, and the wooden ceilings too were blackened from long use.

I placed home-made lamps and some of my favourite pots along the corridor, and at night would come and go between the kitchen and living room in the flickering light, enjoying the cut flowers I put in the pots, and sit late into the night in the small room I had made my study-cum-bedroom, reading books and writing.

Writing . . . this was the most important time of all for me. Even in the house in Fuchu, when I got home from work I would quickly have dinner and then sit down at my desk. I was already used to having time both to work for a living and to write, and I divided my days between these two times. I somehow felt compelled to write, despite a niggling voice questioning what was the point, and even after my husband went to sleep I would sit long into the night with my notebook illuminated only by a desk lamp. And then my world opened to places far removed from daily life, and I came to believe that words had unlimited power.

As I wrote, I would hear the sound of Mii quietly slipping through the bathroom and out through the hole in the lean-to. I glanced up from my manuscript paper and listened briefly for her presence outside, and a blurred shadow moved across the glass doors in front of me. It was Mii walking cautiously on the wall between the house and the shrine.

A timid, unsteady gait. I wondered where she was going.

She used to be so scared of heights . . . In my mind I quietly followed that faint shadow going out into the dark. Was it to the darkness beneath the shrine building, or into the undergrowth of the woodlands all around us? There were no robinias here, but still there was the smell of trees on the breeze.

Mii doubtless followed many paths unknown to me, with ditches and hollows and places that smelled good. Did she play alone or with friends? I didn't know where she went, but all it took was a sense of her presence to conjure up pleasing images of her face as she followed her cat trails, her ears perked up, or the way she walked as she came home satisfied.

I could even hear the sounds of the unknown places

Mii frequented, the sound of the breeze over her head, the rustling of the trees.

She often returned in the morning, her body permeated with a lovely smell. Sometimes bits of leaf mulch were stuck to her back and tail, as though she had been rolling around in grass and dry leaves and on the clayey earth.

When she came home, the first thing she did was go straight to her food bowl in the kitchen. She drank some water, ate her food, groomed herself, and then settled down on the sunny veranda. This was her favourite spot to take a nap.

Once the shade reached the veranda, she would move to the bathroom. Maybe there was some residual warmth left in the bath water, since she would always sleep on the plastic cover over the bathtub in the afternoon.

Now and then she would come home late at night, tired of playing outside. At those times she would avoid me and my husband, and go straight from the kitchen to the bathroom, as though she had her mind on something. She would jump up on to the cover over the still-warm bath water and sleep there until morning.

'Oh, she's back!'

I always knew when Mii came home. She was clumsy, so there would be some sound from the lean-to and bathroom. If she didn't come through to the bedroom, she would be on the bath cover. Going to see her provided a welcome break from my work, and I would tiptoe up to peek in on her. There she would always be, sleeping peacefully.

'So you're home, are you? At least come and say hello!' I would say, and she would look up at me sleepily, then immediately melt back down again.

She looked so soft and happy in those moments. I could gaze for ever at her all curled up in a neat circle with her head and tail tucked in as I wiped up her pawprints in the corridor.

The bath is warm
You on the cover
Curled up, sleeping
Mmm, so toasty
Your back and tail   plump and puffed up
Like a futon aired in the sun
I call you to me but you don't come
You don't come, so I go to you
I just have to boop the tip of your nose as you sleep!

Time flows
Through the cooling bath water
Over you, soft and warm

The two of us indolent
Doing nothing   thinking nothing
Just chuckling softly
Late at night on the cold bathroom floor
Listening to the wind until the water is cold

Mii's Boyfriend

In our first spring after moving to Kokubunji, the garden quince was in flower and the peach tree was blooming.

Mii would roll around on the stones and sand in the garden, and she also learned how to jump up into the peach tree. Until then she had either stayed on the ground or walked along the top of the concrete-block wall, but now she had suddenly got good at jumping. Especially after the branches filled with pink blossoms, she started springing up into them and then back down again. Now and then she would climb up only to find she couldn't come back down and, stuck, she would stand there wailing.

'Come and help me!' she would scream. I pretended not to notice. She screamed louder. I snuck a peek up at the branches, and saw her crouching in a fork halfway up, gripping it tightly with her claws. She must have been taken aback by how high up she'd climbed and become paralysed with fear. It was usually my husband who went to her aid, and if he was home he would always lend her a helping hand. I was the one callously watching from the corridor enjoying her distress, wanting to listen to her sweet, desperate cries for as long as possible.

I wanted to make her cry more, to see her face look even more wretched. Whenever I saw a new expression on her face, I wanted to keep gazing at it until I tired of it.

When nobody came to her rescue, Mii eventually got down by herself, although it would be more accurate to say she fell to a clumsy landing. Each time she would make a sound like *fugyak*, which I found so funny I burst out laughing. She would energetically climb up into the peach tree. After a while I'd hear her crying. A little later there would be another *thump* and *fugyak* as she landed. This kept repeating itself, and I spent my weekends around the spring festival in early March by this peach tree.

One day we had some odd visitors. Several cats sat in a line on top of the wall around our house. A black and white cat, a tabby, and a black cat, all sitting up straight staring at us. I shooed them away and they reluctantly went, but they were soon all back sitting in the same place, yawning or scratching their necks with their hind legs. But they clearly weren't just basking in the sun. It didn't take me long to realise that it was Mii they were after.

In early spring Mii had started restlessly coming and going through the hole in the lean-to. I'd no sooner noticed that she had gone out when she came crashing back in. Then I heard rummaging around the hole followed by a loud screech as though she had crashed into something or had been chased by another cat, and the sound of bits of wood and shovels being knocked over. In the meantime, she dashed back inside looking terrified and breathing heavily.

Mii had come into heat for the first time.

I'd thought she was still so young, but here she was getting her period.

Several weeks before that, the high sharp wails of some cats had reached us on the warm breeze. I wasn't sure where they were coming from, maybe the shrine or the woods or a roof somewhere. Mii had appeared unsettled and restless ever since, but however hard I listened I couldn't distinguish her voice from those of the other cats.

I wasn't concerned about it since I'd gone to where the caterwauling was coming from and Mii hadn't been there. She was such a coward that however much the cats called to her she would only stick her face outside, and at the first hint of trouble she would come dashing straight back in. Even when the amorous duets between male and female cats started up near by, she looked at them as though it had nothing to do with her. Mii was still very kittenlike and kept her distance from the other cats, so it didn't even occur to me to have her spayed.

Before long, though, Mii was frequently coming home screeching loudly and making a lot of noise, crashing into the glass door to the bathroom and falling heavily in the corridor. This was clearly not normal behaviour. Her whole body looked restless, as though floating in space, only her eyes strangely fixed.

Once I heard the sound of footsteps galloping around and went to see what was going on, and saw a cat I didn't know poking his head into the corridor. It was a big black and white male cat. Cats frequently chased each other in and out of the corridor, although I didn't know whether Mii had invited them or they had just barged in of their own accord. The corridor would end up covered in mud, and Mii's fur would stand on end. It was my role to chase out intruders with the broom, and if I heard one when I was working late at night I would grab the broom and charge out into the corridor.

Eventually the male cats seemed to get fed up with the lack of understanding on the part of humans and started sitting in a line on the wall. Mii ignored them all, but she still slipped out at night, which made me think she must have found a cat she liked.

By the end of summer, she was beginning to show some noticeable changes. She wouldn't even look at food that she had practically inhaled before. She lay listlessly on the veranda tossing and turning, and she had grown fat and heavy-looking.

Then she started crouching down in the same place on her bed, often dozing off in that position. But it was only when she stopped eating and drinking for a week that it occurred to me that something was wrong. It happened to be my day off. I observed her carefully for a while then turned her over and got a shock. Something wet was poking its head out from somewhere near her anus. It looked like a grey lump of flesh.

That afternoon, I stuffed Mii into a paper bag, ran out into the street, and hailed a passing taxi. I'd just settled in the seat when I realised I didn't know any veterinary hospitals.

'Take me to a hospital for cats and dogs,' I told the driver, the words tumbling out of me. 'I don't care which one. A hospital for cats and dogs.'

I knew where the pet shops were in central Tokyo, but I didn't have a clue about veterinary clinics. The driver looked taken aback and didn't seem to understand what I was saying. But then he said quietly, 'Ohhh,' as though a light bulb had come on in his head.

He set off, and presently pulled up at a small clinic only about a fifteen-minute walk from my house. I was astonished to find there was one so close to home. I always just travelled between home and work, doing my shopping at a market on the way. I'd never even taken a walk around the neighbourhood, so I hadn't noticed this clinic.

The middle-aged vet took one look at Mii and immediately put her on a drip and set about putting her in position for an X-ray. While waiting for it to process, he stroked her belly, lifted her tail, and raised her eyelids to peer into her eyes. I stood there vacantly watching him.

Soon the X-ray was ready and I got a shock when he held it up to the light and said, 'Oh, it's dead.'

'What do you mean, dead?' What on earth was he talking about?

'It's a very large foetus,' the vet said. 'Cats normally give birth to a few kittens, but she must have only conceived one and it got so big she wasn't able to deliver it.'

Then he said something that defied the imagination: the foetus had started to rot inside her and its bones had punctured her womb in several places. Mii herself had become extremely weak, and even if he operated on her he wasn't sure he could save her.

'I wonder how long she's been like this,' he asked, but I hadn't even realised that she was pregnant and couldn't answer.

'Maybe I should remove her womb. If I remove all of it she might just survive, but I won't know until I try.'

Mii's eyes were restlessly moving around, utterly unlike her normal gaze. They weren't focusing properly, and they lacked strength. Maybe she couldn't even recognise my face any more. I burst into tears. 'Please operate on her,' I tried to say, but my voice caught in my throat and didn't form into proper words.

The operation took almost two hours. Waiting at home, I couldn't help thinking about the line of tomcats sitting on the wall. Which one of them had got Mii pregnant, I wondered. My mind settled on one face. The vet's description of a large foetus led me to think of just one cat, the black and white one, the biggest and ugliest of all the cats hanging around the house. He often dozed on the wall, deftly rolling over to show his fat belly. He was also the one that most often came into the corridor.

He would come so often that whenever I saw him I would tease Mii, 'He's here again, that fatso.' He was so ugly I never dreamed that Mii would fall for him.

He had a large lump on his forehead that made half his face look twisted and reminded me a bit of that fictional swordsman with a slashed eye, Tange Sazen. The white triangle pattern at the base of his neck was like the collar of a kimono, and he looked like a sloppily dressed ronin. His face was round like a tray and his big fat haunches moved jauntily, exuding lust. There was no denying that compared to the others, this black and white cat stood out for his sexual dominance. With his twisted face and sheer intensity, Mii hadn't stood a chance with Tange Sazen.

How come she had fallen for such a delinquent? There must have been a better cat than him! I was every bit as indignant as a mother whose daughter had been swept off by some rogue. I kept watch for that black and white cat, determined to give him a piece of my mind when I found him. Maybe he sensed my mood, though, for Tange Sazen kept his distance all the time Mii was in hospital.

Mii was discharged from hospital a week later. Her belly was raw where it had been shaved and stained yellow with disinfectant, but when I fearfully held her in my arms she made her habitual sweet miaow. Having had her belly cut open and her entire womb removed, Mii was strangely scrawny and forlorn. At first she had to wear a white cone around her neck to stop her from licking her wound and wasn't able to move around much, but after a few days I took it off and she tottered unsteadily around the house, gazing out at the garden through the veranda glass doors as though dazzled by the light.

It was as though Mii had been cured of an evil spirit. Tange Sazen must have sensed that she was back because he once again appeared on top of the wall, but Mii seemed to have learned her lesson and pretended not to see him. Reluctant to give up, Tange Sazen rolled on his back, sending her flirtatious glances. But Mii showed absolutely no interest in going outside.

Mii slept a lot and ate a lot as she convalesced, and as the days passed her face started losing its kittenish features. Her movements were calmer, although that might have been because she was exhausted from the operation. She was eating well and gradually regaining weight, and her face was becoming visibly rounder than before.

Her wound probably hurt, as she would walk a little then lean her head on a step and doze off. I became obsessed with making up for being such a bad cat mum and letting her get pregnant, and I stitched a felt pillow with cotton wadding for her to rest her head on, made a ball-shaped toy she could roll around with, and even let her lap up some raw egg and cream, which I'd never given her before. I'd thought my cat was dying but she'd come back. That alone was enough to make me tear up and to my own dismay I would sit with Mii sobbing my heart out.

'She's still alive so there's nothing to cry about, surely,' my husband said, but I couldn't contain the relief I felt just at the fact that Mii was still here.

'Crying because she didn't die is weird. What would you have done if she had died?'

'I would have cried even more.'

I would tell him things like, 'Today she was walking normally in the corridor,' and, 'Her fur is beginning to grow over her wound,' and cry again.

But however much I cried for joy, Mii would never be able to have kittens. For a while I felt so sorry for her having lost her womb that I would hug her too tightly and she would get fed up and lash out, raising welts on my skin. It didn't hurt, though, since all I could think of was how feeble Mii had looked in the cage at the vet's. And because it was all my fault for not having had her spayed to begin with, and I just wanted to apologise to her all the more.

Soon after this I bought a camera for the first time in my life. I'd never wanted one before and there hadn't been anything I wanted to photograph. However, Mii had undergone big changes in her daily life, and it was no

48

longer enough for me to follow her development with my eyes alone.

My first camera was a Canon A35 Datelux. I had insisted on a camera that could date stamp the photos because the whole point was that I wanted to leave a record of Mii. This camera became our constant companion for almost ten years. I started chasing after her with it, and would sometimes creep up on her when she was asleep and press the shutter.

The Sound of Disintegration

One year passed in the blink of an eye, then three years. The owner of the house still hadn't returned and so we were able to stay. 'We only agreed to two years, but I don't mind you staying on until my son and his family return,' Mr T told us.

I had run into difficulties at work. The second Oil Shock cast a gloom over the construction industry and in the end I had to leave my job, probably because I was the only woman in the workplace. I was unceremoniously dismissed.

What irritated me even more than losing my job was how uncertain I felt about myself afterwards. And my relationship with my husband began to sour around this time. I took things out on him, often snapping at him. The fact I'd lost my job because I was a woman had left a bad taste in my mouth, and I was once again forced to recognise my lack of talent.

I had started out as an interior designer at the time of the 1970 World Expo in Osaka. The whole country was in the grip of a feverish ambition to rise in the world. The period of rapid economic growth was just hotting up, and the enamelware company I worked for was coming into the limelight. I was in the design department of the construction division in the company's Nagoya branch.

I remember all the night-time drinking sessions with the builders, painters and craftsmen, and night after night I would sit on bare concrete floors with these brawny manual workers, blueprints spread out between us, drinking sake out of cups.

I also recall the deeply knowledgeable conversation of the master carpenter K when leaving the worksite late at night, sleepily dispensing gems of wisdom in the passenger seat of the truck, such as, 'When you're hammering in nails, it's best to hold a few in your mouth so you don't have to keep picking them up one by one, and this also makes them sticky with saliva so they don't come out so easily.'

I was always impressed. My admiration for the workers, combined with curiosity, meant that I enjoyed spending time with them and never got bored of being at work.

Being in a bustling worksite was far more interesting than the time spent poring over the blueprints. There were new discoveries to be made every day, and there were also occasionally unexpected hiccups, such as the time when the electrician was doing some last-minute work on cables the night before we were finally due to complete a job, and he put his foot through the ceiling so we ended up working all through the night, or the big fuss when they came to install a mirror only to find my measurements had been out. Despite these and numerous other similar mistakes, over time the blue-prints steadily took on physical form and turned into a space with its own character. Over the course of a few days, a building that had been just grey concrete took on colour and warmth, and was populated with people coming and going.

The sweet smell of fresh paint, the joy of seeing large, freshly polished glass fitted snugly into a window frame, and the thrill when the temporary bare light bulbs were removed and the chandeliers and brand-new electrical appliances were turned on and I would feel like dancing around singing, 'It's done! It's done! Another new place is born!'

The joy I felt in my work continued unabated even after moving to Tokyo. But it's true that I also somehow knew it couldn't continue for ever. The ups and downs of a small design company were relentless, and the volume of work immediately decreased after the Oil Shock hit. I started to feel resigned to the situation, and I sensed that I would be the first to be let go.

And sure enough, that's what happened. The fact it didn't come as a surprise was probably because there was also a sense of relief. Things moved fast in Tokyo. Every time I went to the worksite, I was made to realise how fast trends changed and how cut-throat the competition was. We were often beaten in competitive bids. Tokyo was overflowing with new building materials, paints and construction techniques that I didn't know about and I always had to work hard to brush up my skills so as not to be outdone by other design offices.

And there's one important thing that needs stating. Ever since I'd come to Tokyo, I'd become obsessed with feverishly writing. Back in Nagoya I'd only written poetry, and I still loved poetry best, but since coming to Tokyo I had started to feel more like writing prose.

When I try to analyse what made me start writing prose, all I can say is that I was stimulated by the sheer energy and size of the city. Or maybe I lost my heart to the various facets of the metropolis. The constantly changing daily life like froth spewed out by the city, the speed, the buzz, the smells, all kindled the energy dormant within me into a desire to write. And this desire, with a burning power I had not felt for years, mushroomed into an urge to express myself in the here and now of the place.

The shadows here, the sounds there, the changes, the people . . . I wanted to get to know it all. I began intently observing people on the street and the bawdy face of the city behind them, and I started writing about it in prose, not poetry.

I had started writing when I was still in elementary school and had soon become the type of child who always had her nose stuck in a book.

Back then, one of the books I was crazy about was *Little Women*. I found all of the four girls in it charming, but the one I liked best was the second sister, Jo, maybe for her strong-minded, cool disposition, or maybe because she was obsessed with writing. My little sister's favourite was the youngest, Amy, but I vehemently rejected this and envied Jo for having a place in the attic where she could write. This might have been because I was vaguely thinking that I too wanted to write. I began to hanker after Jo's writing space, and so I looked around for one of my own and settled on the upper floor of an outhouse in my family home.

Our home was a typical farmhouse with a number of interlocking tatami rooms. They were all on one level, and when you removed all the fusuma doors between them, they made one large room like you get in onsen hotels. This was not conducive to feeling relaxed enough to write. I wanted the atmosphere of a den. Luckily for me, the upstairs of the outhouse was a bit like a cave, with low beams barely above head height. What's more, it was full of old pickle barrels of various sizes, equipment for dyeing cloth, and various farming tools and machinery lying around, which cast all kinds of mysterious shadows around the room.

The moment I came home from school I would race up to that dusty, dimly lit space. It was accessed not by a staircase but by a rickety old ladder made from bits of wood knocked together, but once you were up there the world below completely disappeared. Even when my parents called me, I didn't answer. It wasn't that I was deliberately ignoring them, just that when I was up there all sounds from below really did fade away.

My desk was a stack of mikan orange crates, and my chair was an old tub. I put a clean cloth over the crates, and a cotton-stuffed futon over the tub, and wrote diligently in my notebook like a fully fledged writer. I was really like the girls in *Little Women* when they were absorbed in playing pilgrims from *The Pilgrim's Progress*.

Once I started writing, the outside world vanished. Instantly my dormant inner world was shaken awake. Through a small high window, clouded by dust, I could see a bright green bamboo grove. When I was at my desk, this small bamboo grove, only about twenty tsubo, in my daydreams became a forest on a plateau. The breeze in the bamboos became a howling wind. In my imagination the landscape swelled and suddenly the bamboo grove was an oasis in a desert on the other side of the world.

How many years had passed since then? I'd been so absorbed with my design work that I had become distanced from writing. Now it became an internal voice, a vibration that roused me. That delightful den and the dream space that knew no limits. I want to write, I thought. I want to go back to those times. Something about it shook me to the core. I was even almost convinced that I had long been waiting for this very moment.

It was probably high time for me to be sacked from my job.

On sunny days I would lie on the veranda reading a book. If Mii came to join me, I would play with her. She stuck close to me, unused to having me there during the day, and when I was at my desk writing she would be at my feet, purring loudly. Seeing her there out of the corner of my eye, I asked myself any number of times what I wanted to do with my life. And first and foremost, I wanted to write. In order to do so, I had to buy time. And to buy time, I had to make money . . .

Ever since I'd left home ten years earlier, I had never once been out of work. It had become second nature, an ingrained habit. It was natural for a couple to both be earning a living, and I'd always wanted to work. I didn't think I'd be able to make money from my writing straight away, but in any case I could just not see myself being at home without a job.

Two months had gone by with me spending all my time reading books or writing in my notebook when an older woman friend said to me, 'If you're not doing anything else, come and work for us. Part-time is okay too.'

And so, after having been holed up for a while in the quietness of the Kokubunji house, I ventured back out. My new workplace was the small publishing house where my friend worked. My job was to sort manuscripts and assist her with editorial matters.

While I kept one ear out for the sound of Mii slipping outside at night, I was no longer fazed by anything that came into the house. The sound of Mii's 'male friends' running around the corridor and Mii's voice overreacting to them all felt somehow distant, as though I was hearing it in a dream. When I turned my back on the presence of the cats fighting and frolicking and sat down at my manuscript paper, new worlds opened up there one after another and it felt like the night could go on for ever.

The fact that Mii was unable to breed was another reason for the nights being longer. Thankfully I didn't have to worry about Mii's soft womb harbouring kittens from some unknown father, or pity her for being lonely either.

Mii was by now settled in the house and familiar with the woods. She enjoyed playing with the stray cats and came in and out as she pleased. Just hearing the wails of the cats in the grounds of the shrine or the sound of them crawling through the hole in the lean-to by the bathroom and running about the house was enough to bring a smile to my lips. The physiology and instincts of these lively, young and supple, utterly uninhibited creatures enriched my nights. Mii was as cowardly as ever among the Kokubunji cats that did as they pleased, but still she went outside. And she would quietly leave the house as though gauging that it was time for me to work.

I would stroke her head, roll her on the floor, fondle

her paw beans, and when I was reading blow on her ears. Sometimes after playing with her for a while, I would say, 'That's your lot,' and she seemed to understand, for she would suddenly stop and go out into the hall and crawl through the hole into the big outside world. Meanwhile, I would chronicle everything in a world in which all sound had disappeared far away, now and then ripping up manuscript pages with a sigh.

It was 1980 when my husband and I started living apart. He always came home very late at night, no doubt because he was so busy at work, but then one day he was transferred to Osaka. He probably felt like going alone, having grown tired of having a wife who spent all her time writing, her hair in a mess. For my part, I had lost track of the minutiae of daily life. And so, without even asking him what he wanted me to do, I bundled him off to Osaka and sat back down at my desk as always.

And then later the same year, a story I had finally finished led to a fresh start. The work I had written in Mii's company night after night unexpectedly won a prize for new writers in a well-known magazine. Given that winning a prize was the way writers broke into the scene in Japan, this was a seismic occasion. At the same time, I had lost the closeness of life with my husband, and was beginning to feel the draught around my feet. When I sat at my desk, books open before me, the guilt of being alone in Tokyo began to well up in me like spring water.

What was I choosing and what was I throwing away?

What had I wanted to achieve by packing my husband off alone to Osaka?

I couldn't see my own future prospects. And yet, all I wanted to do was write fiction. At the same time, I was trying to find meaning in remaining alone in Tokyo. Writing fiction was surely something I could do anywhere. However, I just could not see myself being anywhere but Tokyo. The life force of this huge metropolis stirred something dormant within me, drew out words, and gave me a sense of being at one with the city. I was crazy about the place, as though I had met a man like no other I had ever known. The way it was brimming over with people, the buzz, the speed . . .

There was such a thing as a meaningful solitude. I wanted to believe this. If I didn't, the ground would crumble under my feet. I had to hold on to the belief that writing fiction would be the departure that would bolster me. In order to discover meaning and a reason for my existence in writing fiction, I decided to invest all the prize money into publishing one last collection of poetry. I had to abandon the poetry that I had stuck to all these years to convince myself I was embarking on something new.

The title of this poetry collection was *The Sound of Disintegration*. When I think about my state of mind at the time, there was also something profoundly meaningful in that. I have the feeling that I was unconsciously listening to the sound of disintegration within myself, too.

On my days off, I would take lots of photos of Mii. Mii sleeping, Mii on top of the concrete-block wall listening intently, Mii climbing up on to the branches of the peach tree then losing her nerve and falling down, Mii quietly climbing on to my desk, sitting with her head beside the warm light bulb and gazing at me.

The camera became my only means of capturing the time that passed me by. The quiet time with just Mii and myself. The sound of the shutter in the morning, the blue-white flash that lit up the room at night. Mii still didn't understand what it was I was holding in my hand, and when I called her she would look at me, and I captured her in the finder. Sometimes when I was working at night she would jump up on to my desk and model for me.

She would plonk herself down on my manuscript paper, gleefully interrupting my work. Or she would sit right in the middle of the morning newspaper. That way she could get me to play with her. She loved being wrapped in paper like a sushi roll and tumbled around the floor. She would stare up at my face, innocently believing that just by sitting on the newspaper she could get me to play that game with her.

At other times she would bury herself inside a large paper bag from a department store or market and call to me. When I flicked or scratched the outside of the bag, she would lash out with her claws from inside the bag at the place the sound was coming from. She had so much fun searching for that sound! When she was really pestering me a lot I would hang the bag with her still in it on a clothes hook on the wall and get back on with my work, ignoring her there.

On those nights and weekends without my husband, I would turn my camera on Mii pestering me to play in order to forget about him.

Nights in Musashino

I had been living separately from my husband for about two years. I would walk aimlessly around the neighbourhoods of Kokubunji and Kunitachi. I was usually with someone or other.

Putting out a poetry collection had been my way of burying my poetry in order to focus on prose, but it didn't quite turn out the way I'd intended. Through my publisher I had come to know about several poetry magazines and had become acquainted with some young poets and artists. Or it might have been that although I was insisting on abandoning poetry, a part of me was still somehow clinging on to it. I knew a lot more literary magazine editors after receiving the prize, but I was also getting to know people connected to poetry at the same rate.

I was still in limbo, loitering around the entrance to fiction. Not long after my husband left, I started dropping by a bar frequented by poetry friends and ending up on the last train home.

After leaving work, I would wander around the neighbourhoods along the Chuo Line. From Shinjuku to

Koenji, Koenji to Kunitachi, Kunitachi to Kokubunji, my feet would take me away from home seeking music and conversation.

I knew a lot of people at a bar called P in Koenji. Jazz played in this bar with its black-and-white sharp-edged design, and the owner, Y, was also a poet. We would sit on cold chairs listening to Albert Ayler and Miles Davis. One night the melancholy strains of Casals's 'Song of the Birds' that someone had brought in might be playing, while on other nights we might hear the soulful voice of Billie Holiday.

Around that time I would often catch sight of the author Kenji Nakagami in a coffee shop outside Kunitachi Station. There was always an air of tension, as though he was meeting his editor or delivering a manuscript, and for the first time I was struck by the sheer presence exuded by an established author. Although I had been fortunate enough to receive a prize, I was stuck at a standstill, unable to move on to the next step. I still couldn't see what it was I wanted to write, and was just going round and round in circles.

My lifestyle had undergone big changes. I hungered for people and for music. I absolutely identified with expressive people, and just had to be meeting someone all the time. Looking back, I have no idea what we used to talk about when I was hanging out in my favourite bars. I would do the rounds of the jazz cafes in Kokubunji and the live jazz club in the ginkgo-tree-lined avenue in

Kunitachi (this place, with its pitch-black walls and bare pipes in the ceiling, was reminiscent of Soho in New York City), and end up going home roaring drunk.

Nights in Kokubunji were chilly. It was at least one or two degrees lower than central Tokyo. When my body started getting cold, so did my heart, and there were times when the tears would naturally come as I made my way home.

I didn't know what my husband's apartment in Osaka was like. I had never been there, but this was partly because on his periodic visits home he would tell me, 'You'd better not come. You'll only be disappointed.' When night fell, I was gripped by a melancholy, wistful image of him alone in that flat.

I could already see that by not going to see my husband in Osaka and spending my days with my head full of words I was callously discarding something. But while the tears flowed thick and fast in my drunken stupor, they were so pitiful that I clung all the more on to words.

Unable to contain my feelings and desperate to write, sitting at my desk did not bury the sense of loss. Even though my body was severely flushed with alcohol, my muddled mind was quite clear. My husband and I were growing further and further apart. I knew that it wasn't because of the physical distance between Osaka and Tokyo, but a distance that had emerged in my heart and was steadily growing. When I was with my husband I was always thinking of something else, and even when he was talking I would just be gazing at his lips without knowing what he was saying. And while he realised this, he didn't say anything.

It was clear that I was destroying the life my husband and I had made together. Consumed with guilt, in order to forget I started drinking heavily, and I would often run along the streets at night and fall over. Maybe because I'd been drinking I never felt pain, just a jarring impact. I tripped over stones, stumbled on dips in the path, fell down steps, and I often got home to see in the light that my stockings were ripped to pieces and my knees and arms covered in blood.

What was comforting was the sight of Mii patiently waiting for me in the dark.

Wherever she was when she heard the sound of footsteps, Mii would come dashing through the gap in the garden gate and coil herself around my feet. I could hear in the way her voice broke and became shrill that she had been desperate to see me. Sometimes her body was terribly cold, as though she had been playing in the grounds of the shrine, and other times she was strangely warm, maybe having been asleep on the cover over the bath. When I picked her up in my arms, she would always lick my face as though to welcome me home, from my cheeks to my eyelids, and from my eyelids to my forehead.

Any number of times I stood stock-still in the entrance

to my house, giving myself over to the warmth and slow, steady movements of my cat's tongue. Holding her like that for some time, close to tears, the blood started flowing back through my chilled heart, and with it feeling returned to my body and for the first time I noticed the pain of my wounds.

My days were completed by these night-time cuddles with Mii. Whatever the day, it ended seamlessly like this. Late at night I would open a tin of horse mackerel or bonito cat food, and I never tired of watching her scarfing it down. I would squat beside her, crouched on the floor with her head tucked in, utterly at ease, absorbed in the sight of her active mouth rhythmically eating her food and the sound of her chewing.

Then, in the light of the pale green lamp, I would wash my wounds, apply antiseptic, have something to eat, and read a book. In that quiet time, both the weariness from a day's work and my shame and embarrassment at my ridiculous injuries began to fade, and I would suddenly find myself gazing absently into Mii's face.

And at that moment I would murmur to myself, 'I'm such an idiot,' and feel like laughing. How absurd I was with my arms and legs flailing wildly without even knowing who to flail at . . .

At the same time, I could see how obsessed I was with the idea of fiction. I realised how I could only see what was dangling before my eyes. It was a chilling feeling accompanied by a kind of guilt, but I just couldn't shake it however hard I tried. It was always Mii who soothed these endless circular emotions that went nowhere.

When I slipped into bed, Mii would also crawl in with me. She would use my arm as a pillow and I would stroke her back, making up for not being there during the day, and that seemed to be enough to reassure her as I would sometimes notice her lying beside me with her paws neatly aligned, snoring faintly. Having made sure I was asleep, she sometimes would slip outside, maybe wanting to play more or maybe going to meet a boyfriend.

Mii had decided sometime before that a cardboard box with a soft mat inside it was her own bedroom, and since I had started putting the box next to my pillow she would alternate between sleeping in her room and in my bed. Sometimes I would open my eyes in the middle of the night and, seeing her in it, would gaze into her eyes for no particular reason. Even when I was lying on my stomach in bed reading a book, sometimes Mii's face was there right in front of my nose and she would be staring at me.

When I called 'Mii' she would always answer *mya* and then leave her tongue sticking out as if she'd forgotten to put it away. She would sit there for ages with this cute little pink blep, so I would often tease her by sticking out my tongue too. On those nights I discovered that human tongues were nowhere near as pretty as cats' tongues.

As my relationship with my husband was breaking

down, Mii was in the middle of it all with me, innocently unaware of what was on my mind. Had she been human, she would have grumbled and clashed with me, but she didn't say anything and nor did I. Maybe it was the shared warmth of our animal bodies that made communication between us possible? Or maybe the fact we couldn't communicate in words cushioned us and kept things calm between us.

Whenever we were together, we ate in the same room, we lay on our bellies on the floor of the warm veranda, gazed at the light shining on the green of the trees, and dozed off. Neither of us said anything. Yet neither of us felt in the slightest uncomfortable.

On the contrary, when I was sleeping next to Mii, I had the feeling that I too had become a cat. Since my husband had left, Mii and I had become closer than ever. Our intimacy was spun without words and in time formed into an unbreakable bond. We slept in the same bed, entrusting our bodies to each other, snuggling together, and in the morning the first thing we saw was each other.

> *Birds fly   the wind howls   through the big,*
> *   dark, forest*
> *I walk   not with my feet   but with my eyes*
> *Listening   if I divine where you are going*
> *My toes too get wet   and my nose grows damp*

I don't really want to be a cat but
I rapturously imagine what you see
Where cats go in Musashino's dark open spaces
What is lurking there what you smell there
I read so many books but I know so little
You walk in that world unknown to me and
When you come home
As if trying to teach me something
You clatter your little food bowl

Where do   cats go   night after night?
From the distant night that humans cannot see
You come home   with cold feet   your ears pointed

I wipe clean   small footprints in the corridor
Traces of the night
The remains of a secret that is yours alone

Farewell, You Woods

In 1983 I found myself walking around Tokyo clutching a map. Not so much walking as running, because otherwise I wouldn't be in time. At the end of March I had gone to visit my landlord as always with my rent money inserted in my rent book and in the hushed entrance Mrs T said in the same calm tones as the previous month, 'It seems my son and his family are transferring back to Tokyo, so I'm afraid I have to ask you to leave the house.'

I had always known this day would come. I was ready for it, but still when it came to the crunch I couldn't get my head around it right away. Mrs T said she could wait until the end of May, but I didn't see how I could find a new house by then. It was only two months away. How was I going to fit in house-hunting around work?

'It's a good opportunity for you to move to Osaka, isn't it?' my friend at work said. Osaka, Osaka! I pictured the unknown apartment where my husband still lived alone. If I went there, it would probably be my salvation. But what exactly would I be saved from? The desperate situation I was in? Finding somewhere for me and my cat to go? My husband was a kind person, but if I went to Osaka we would have to rebuild our lives together from scratch. I would probably have to abandon everything I had gained in Tokyo, my friends, my job, my time at night, and maybe even Mii.

My body was constantly on edge with this feeling of being cornered. Freedom! There was something I had to be free from. Freedom alone could save me. I now became obsessed with the thought of it. Wasn't it in order to be free that I had chosen to work for a living, to stay alone with my cat, and follow the life of a writer even knowing it may never come to anything? Freedom was also the pleasure I gained in exchange for the inconveniences that bound me. So shouldn't I maintain this freedom despite all the many inconveniences?

As long as my husband allowed me to, I could stay in Tokyo for ever. Effectively neglecting and abandoning him. But that was morally reprehensible. I couldn't go on living with a broken heart, putting on a brave face.

'We must split up.' It had hit me suddenly, but I felt as if the decision had long been made. I knew that once I said it out loud there would be no going back, but still I couldn't resist the urge to say it.

'You're always charging on ahead,' my husband said. 'And that's why you get lost, isn't it? I can't bear the thought of you like that, but that's the sort of person you are so there's not much I can do about it. It was the same when you said you wanted to write fiction. All I can do is write, you said. That really scared me, but your mind was all set and there was no room for anyone else.'

I was the sort of wife who never talked much. The sort of wife who preferred to spend her time reading than talking. The sort of wife who, if she had time to watch TV after dinner, would prefer to sit down at her desk. And also the sort of wife who would slip into her own world and linger endlessly there without coming out. My husband had given that sort of wife her freedom when he had gone alone to Osaka, but while he was away I had wilfully set off at a run and soon became a woman who had lost sight of her husband.

'Once you've made up your mind that's all there is to it, I suppose,' my mother said on the other end of the phone. 'You're the very epitome of a headstrong fool. That's just how you are. You've always been like that. Once you've made up your mind about something there's no going back.'

Having said much the same as my husband, she wept. 'I'm more sorry for your husband having to bear the brunt of your choice than I am for you,' she said through her tears.

But I was not in the slightest moved by their laments, and had no intention of changing my mind. Instead, I just charged headlong into living alone. The first thing I had to do was to find a house where Mii and I could live together. I couldn't rely on anyone else. It was up to me alone to make a space for us to live in. I would make sure of this fresh start.

And there was no question of me ever getting someone else to take Mii in or look after her, and I could never abandon her. This cat was mine, my precious partner, and I had to keep her whatever happened. If I abandoned her, something in me really would collapse. That's how I felt.

People could at least think about how to make a living, physically and mentally. But animals that had been domesticated by people, that were used to being fed by the person who had raised them, could no longer return to the wild. I simply could not see my timid little cat toughing it out among all the strays.

It's also possible that while I was determined to leave my husband, I was scared of living on my own. I probably wanted to have Mii waiting patiently for me as a last bastion, a warm refuge in our new home.

That was definitely true. I needed to convince myself that I wasn't alone.

From previous experience I knew that it wouldn't be easy to find a place where Mii and I could live together, but it was even more futile and exhausting than I had imagined. I spent all my breaks at work, and all my days off, calling around estate agents I found in newspaper and magazine ads, and any that sounded even remotely responsive I immediately went to see them and looked through their property files.

But there was nothing! There were no houses anywhere where I could live together with my cat.

A house with a garden. Somewhere with a lot of green. A rent I could afford, ideally a detached house with holes in it. It could even have a straw-thatched roof. I didn't care how old it was. I didn't even mind if it was falling apart. As long as it had easy access for a cat.

The moment I mentioned that last condition, the estate agent would give a thin smile or look at me pityingly. There weren't any houses like that these days, I was told, although I might find the odd one on the very outskirts of Tokyo or for double the rent. I was also told in tones that could be either kindly or cruel, I couldn't tell, that my choices were limited because of my cat, so perhaps I should consider abandoning her or finding someone else to take her in.

I refused to set foot again in that sort of estate agent, and my anger doubled by the day. Eventually, with no outlet for that anger it turned to wretchedness, and I dreaded looking in the mirror on my days off. Would I come home looking miserable today, too? Driven even further into a corner after a fruitless search? I could just see it.

My anger was not confined to estate agents alone. I felt hatred for the whole of Tokyo, mistrusted anyone who didn't keep pets, and felt animosity towards those able to live in houses that allowed cats or who could solve everything with money.

What was so bad about cats? Humans weren't everything. How impoverished this huge wonderful energised city called Tokyo was by the fact it had nowhere where humans and cats could live together! I became full of resentment, distrust and sadness, and every day I walked around town in a rage.

Thinking back, that anger and sadness must be why I could not remember anything about the neighbourhoods I walked around (and there must have been many, since I spent every minute of every day off searching). I was disappointed at constantly being accommodated in ways irrelevant to me, being told a place was okay for children or how I could even have a piano there, but this just stoked up more anger in me and made me all the more determined to find somewhere to live with my cat.

Then one day (it was already April by then) I was in an estate agent's office in Shibuya, at my wits' end as always. They didn't have anywhere that allowed pets and was within my budget. I didn't want to despair at being disappointed yet again. But in spite of myself, waves of despair were lapping at my feet. I was on the verge of being washed away when the estate agent said nonchalantly, 'Perhaps you should consider buying a place?'

Dumbfounded, I stared at him across the counter. It had never once occurred to me to buy my own place, so for a moment I thought he must be talking to someone else. But he explained that if you owned a place, the issue of pets was much easier than with rentals.

'But I don't have any money,' I said.

He tapped a few keys on his calculator, briskly calculating the lowest down payment, the amount I could afford to pay back every month on my salary, and so forth.

'If you can make a down payment of three million yen, the monthly payments on a second-hand condo costing ten million yen will work out at roughly the same as your current rent, or maybe even a little less.'

I leaned forward and peered at the calculator. I didn't care if it was just a sales pitch or a trap. The words 'if you buy a flat you can live with your cat' were seared into my head and wouldn't go away.

If I had enough for the down payment, I could get somewhere for Mii and myself to live. So shouldn't I consider buying? I had no experience of either borrowing money or taking out a loan, but having only considered rental properties until now it felt as though a fog had lifted and my mood lightened.

So that was it, all I had to do was buy a flat! That was also a possibility.

From that day on, I didn't want to see another rental property. Instead, I flicked through the files of apartments for sale. There were so many! Tokyo was inundated with second-hand apartments. And strangely enough, the floor plans of all these apartments for sale looked so much grander than any of the rental properties I had seen.

The agent, S, searched for suitable properties for

me and contacted me frequently. Each time, I went to view the apartment he suggested, in places like Shibuya, Koenji, Inokashira Park. By now I was of a mind to use up all my savings. But it was still not enough, so I would have to somehow borrow the rest from my mother or someone. Once I made this decision, I was full of anticipation at being able to live with Mii and in high spirits even knowing it would leave me penniless.

But I didn't find anywhere I liked right away. I viewed apartments where the commute to work would have taken too long, apartments that needed a lot of money spent on renovation before being liveable, and apartments that had little sunlight and looked claustrophobic. There were also properties that were way over my budget.

We were almost into May when S contacted me about a property in Shinagawa. Shinagawa? I kept looking at the map of Tokyo. I only knew Shinagawa as a stop on the bullet train I took from Tokyo to Nagoya where my mother lived. I had never set foot in the place before. And unlike the other properties I had viewed up to now, this flat was in a tall building.

Looking at the floor plan, it was not exactly large at just 10 tsubo, but it was a corner apartment with east- and north-facing windows. The price was a little over ten million yen. If I could make the down payment, the mortgage repayments would be considerably lower than the rent I paid in Kokubunji.

It was a warm afternoon when I alighted in Shinagawa

for the first time ever and went to view the flat. It was small, but well maintained. It was clean and bright, and what's more it felt breezy and spacious. The couple who owned it didn't have children, and had been living in it since soon after it was built. When I saw how well they had looked after it, with no pin holes in the walls, well-polished windows, and not a single trace of grease on the kitchen walls, I knew this was the one.

I made up my mind on the spot. Timewise I couldn't afford to dither any more, and I didn't have the energy to keep looking further. I turned a blind eye to the fact it was next to a main road, and was on the very edge of Tokyo in an area that was largely on reclaimed land. My only regret was that it was not the house with holes for Mii to come and go that I had longed for. It was on the fifth floor, with no open area or park for her to play in. It was an apartment floating in space, nothing like the house in Kokubunji. But there was no going back. As long as we could live here together, it would do. I could worry about keeping Mii entertained once I'd got somewhere for us to live.

When I got home to Kokubunji, I told Mii about it. I told her there were no woods there, that it wasn't on the ground, that there weren't any holes for her to go outside like she was used to, that she wouldn't be able to go out for walks at night any more, but also that I had searched high and low for somewhere and had reached my limit.

We would just have to find new games to play. I would

definitely find a new way. As I stroked Mii's head, I wasn't sure whether my mood was happy or sad. But if I let this one get away, there wouldn't be anywhere for us to go.

The next few weeks were a blur of activity. I prepared necessary documents like my residence and seal registration certificates, and worked on getting the money I needed together. S explained the procedures for getting a mortgage but I still didn't understand them and left everything up to him. I could look at my bank book as often as I wanted, there was still no money left in my account.

Be that as it may, I had found somewhere for us to live. It was wonderful to have a place where we could settle down, even if I was completely broke. It would take me twenty years to pay off the mortgage, but as long as I was in good health I would pay it off. And for the moment I had a job that would at least keep us in food. I had never been so grateful for my good health. If things really became impossible, then I would figure it out when the time came.

'We'll manage somehow. It'll work out.'

Now that the apartment had been decided I was full of optimism, and every time I went home to the house in Kokubunji the first thing I did was cuddle Mii. I would hold her and tell her over and over again, 'We're moving to a new home. We have to leave here, but I know you'll like the new place. You will try, won't you?'

Meanwhile, Mii kept coming and going through the hole in the lean-to and the bathroom she loved so much.

Before long, she wouldn't be able to crawl through holes any more so I wanted her to make the most of it while she could. I took her out to the shrine and the ginkgo woods just to listen to the wind.

Ten more days, one week, three days . . . Counting down the days until we had to leave this old house, I stood outside gazing at it. I crouched in the darkness and rolled Mii around on the earth steeped with the smell of leaves until late at night. She rolled on her back showing her belly and cried innocently, 'Do it again!', not realising why I was doing it so much.

On 12 May my husband and I were formally divorced. And on 30 May, the contract for my mortgage was approved.

I had lost one place, and was moving to another. This was not a change of direction, it was a natural transition. It was a new departure with no thought of whether I could do it or not, or whether it was for better or for worse. Just as my husband had said, I would set off at a run and then get lost. I knew he was right, but I couldn't stop myself.

The final farewell between my husband and me took place not when the divorce papers came through, but when I moved. He came from Osaka to help me, packed up his few belongings, and lastly stroked Mii's head and said, 'Well, then.'

We had met in our high school days, somehow fallen in love, and lived together for over ten years depending on the warmth of each other's bodies, and this was our farewell. There was nothing more to be said. I went to Shinagawa, he went to Osaka.

Even if we saw each other after that, we were no longer a couple.

From tomorrow it's the two of us   when I told
*   you this*
You answered
The two of us is good   myaa myaa
Even if you didn't really understand   as though you did
You answered

Your chest puffed up
Your soft, happy body
As night falls you go out   when morning comes you
*   return*
I don't know where you go, but
I'm sure you go to the bottom of the world
To a place shining   with wind and water and light

That world   will it still exist tomorrow?
Even with just the two of us   will it still exist?
Gazing at the small hole you crawl through
I crouch down
Waiting for the nights that start from tomorrow

Revolution!   a rebel army of two

3

A Fresh Start

Sea and a Night View

Shinagawa was a strange neighbourhood. It was on the edge of Tokyo, and was also a border post along the old Tokaido highway during the Edo period. Back then, upon seeing the distance marker indicating 2 ri from Nihonbashi in the city centre, travellers must have prepared their mindset according to whether they were departing for Kyoto or arriving in the capital from Kyoto.

I sometimes wondered whether it was to soothe the travellers' each and every emotion that there were so many temples on the Tokaido. They stood at intervals as though marking out a strong, steady rhythm along this once spirited but now dull road, their broad roofs lit up by sunlight.

When I first came to Shinagawa, I was taken aback by how quiet this former highway was on Sundays. The moment I stepped out of my apartment and went downstairs, I was engulfed in the continuous noise and bustle of traffic on Yamate Dori and the Dai-ichi Keihin National Highway. But the moment I stepped into the Kaido everything fell quiet despite it being a shopping street.

This former post town had been the gateway to Edo. It had been teeming with people and horses and lodging places, a place where meetings and farewells intermingled. That was long gone. In Shinagawa now, the area around the station was cheerful and bright, but once you stepped away from that, you were enveloped in the sombre atmosphere of the shitamachi in a warren of narrow streets, the old brick walls of a public bathhouse, and deserted alleyways hemmed in by black fences and concrete-block walls. At the end of a narrow street in a part of the city that appeared stuck in time stood an empty apartment house covered in ivy, maybe already bought up by developers.

The apartment block where I was now living was close to the Meguro River. The building jutted skywards, tall enough to be noticeable even in those surroundings. Eleven floors in height, it had been built in 1971 and was said to have stood out even more back then.

In front of it was the highway and beyond that a temple complex, thanks to which there wasn't a single other tall building near by and the view had hardly changed since it was built. Behind it were the hilly upmarket residential areas of Gotenyama and Ikedayama, notable for their detached houses and expensive low-rise flats.

In Kokubunji there hadn't been such a discernible difference in the height of the landscape. It had just been an expanse of damp earth and green. But it wasn't only the landscape that was different. First I had to get used to the noise.

This part of town was really noisy. If it was only the sound of the traffic it wouldn't be so bad, but there was a fire station next door and fire engines and ambulances would suddenly turn on their sirens and rush out. I got a shock the first time I heard that sound in the middle of the night. On top of that, the highway outside was a favourite route for the bosozoku biker gangs at night. They would race past, engines screaming, on their way to the area of reclaimed land occupied by wharfs and warehouses.

Coming from the greenery of Kokubunji filled with the natural sounds of the wind and rustling of the trees, to begin with I didn't know what to make of this neighbourhood utterly devoid of greenery. It was a whitish rusty brown, a stone-grey place. This was my impression from the one time I saw the view from the roof when I first moved in. Normally there was no access to the roof, but I begged the caretaker to unlock it just that once for me to see, and the sky that day was overcast, making the whole place look milky-smoky.

I was first astonished by how high the building was, the magnificent view far into the distance, and the strength of the wind, and then utterly captivated by the sight of a glittering line beyond. The shallow waters of Tokyo Bay.

I could see the pale brown of the sea. It was the first

time I'd ever seen the sea in all the years I'd lived in Tokyo. A whitish brown . . . that was my Shinagawa.

I had only ever lived in the suburbs and could not imagine living in the heart of the metropolis, but little by little I got to know it and gradually came to like it. As a working woman, I was grateful to have such a central place to live, and however late it was, as long as you were within the circular loop of the Yamanote Line, it never took too long to get home.

The first time I saw the night view from my apartment, it took my breath away! Gotenyama blocked my view of Shinagawa Station, but I had a wide-open vista over Tokyo Bay. The sea wasn't visible from the fifth floor, but at night the lights from buildings dotted here and there sparkled, and I never got tired of gazing out at them, especially in the rain. Some nights I wanted to see the view from higher up, and so I would go up and down the emergency stairs in search of a view.

And oh, I could see Tokyo Tower! And the lounge bars of big hotels! The view from the upper floors was quite different from that on the fifth floor.

I gained many things upon moving here. I had lost the damp earth and green forests, but now height and the glow from distant windows and the wind and the sky had entered my vision. It was a huge, unfettered sight. A new landscape, mineral and worldly, that I hadn't been able to see when I was close to the damp earth of Kokubunji. They were all mine now.

And so, day by day I discovered new things and grew accustomed to the hills and the views, but what did Mii make of it all? I will never forget the wary look on her face when we moved in. After everything was done, I finally let her out of the cupboard and she froze in bewilderment, her eyes tense and drawn, not knowing which way to turn.

There was no trace of the familiar smells of the corridor or veranda or woods. I could see just how shocked she was at finding herself in this unfamiliar place.

On the day we moved, I wrapped Mii up in a big towel and placed her in a brand-new wicker carrier, then got into the removal company's truck. Mr and Mrs T came out to see me off after saying goodbye and, having never let on to them that I was keeping a cat in their house, I didn't want them to catch sight of Mii.

The truck was parked in the shrine grounds. As I got in, I glanced around the garden that Mii had loved playing in, the garden where we had basked in the sun together, the garden with a peach tree that had small pink blossoms. In one corner, I saw a pot with a dried-up plant that I had forgotten all about lying on its side.

The only things I left behind were that old plant pot and the scratch marks Mii had left on the sliding door to the kitchen. She seemed to like the feel of that door, and even though I'd given her numerous scratch pads she would always gleefully sharpen her claws on it. I tried to stop her but she just went at it even more brazenly so eventually I gave up and let her do as she pleased, and she quickly shredded it.

Overnight she had lost everything that had been part of her daily life. She looked around the new apartment as if surveying it, and looked up at me. The first thing she did was to sniff everything in sight in this unfamiliar place littered with cardboard boxes.

She spent that whole night creeping around with her nose glued to the floor, searching for anything that might have her smell. The dark vinyl flooring, the blue tiles in the bathroom, and the solid sash windows that blocked the noise outside, the books I had only just put up on the shelves, and the mat in the kitchen. Finally coming across this mat infused with her smell, she timidly yet scrupulously sniffed it all over.

There was another object in the flat that Mii was familiar with: the beige upholstered chair. She loved the hollow in its seat. When she'd tired of napping on the veranda or on the bathtub cover, she would jump on to this chair and fall asleep. I put her favourite stuffed toy jaguar on to it for her. I had received the jaguar as a free gift soon after we moved to Kokubunji, and it became Mii's sole playmate when I wasn't home. She would grab its ear and drag it all over the house, and sometimes she would lick it all over. Occasionally I would catch sight of her sleeping with her head on its belly, like a mother and child. As well as Mii's precious chair and playmate,

I had brought her cardboard box bedroom that she'd used in Kokubunji. Mii sniffed it, then got in it as though there was nothing else she could do, but still unable to settle she got up again and continued prowling endlessly around the flat. She was probably looking for a way out. That night she didn't stop walking sorrowfully around the tiny apartment, while I couldn't sleep for the sound of the traffic.

After Summer, Autumn

Slowly, slowly, Mii got used to living in our small apartment. Now that she couldn't go outside, her new play area was inside the cupboard. I left it open for her, and she would jump up on to the middle shelf then back down again. Sometimes she would squeeze herself into the darkness behind the futon I kept in there, playing hide-and-seek by herself.

But of course she might have been searching for the hole she used to crawl through to go outside. In the middle of the night, I would hear her energetically sharpening her claws on the cardboard scratchpad when she was irritable, or dragging her toy jaguar around.

In summer, Mii liked to go out on to the balcony when night fell, and she wandered around in the shadow of the washing machine and squeezed between the plant pots. I had fixed some bamboo screens up around the railings to make sure she couldn't slip and fall off by mistake, and she would press her head up against them trying to see outside. I was sure that she recalled the sensations of summer, and that she was remembering the cedar and ginkgo trees in Kokubunji, although the smell of the breeze and the colour of the sky here were quite different.

As I watched her, I recalled how she used to become more feral in spring and summer. Many a time I had come home from work and turned on the light, then screamed upon seeing her crouched next to a barely alive fieldmouse or lizard. She would nimbly roll it over with her front paw and jump back, then poke it and spring back again, so quick and proud of herself. A cruel expression hovered around her small mouth as she kept looking up at her dumbstruck human as though to say, 'See how clever I am!'

Once there was a large pigeon with its wing chewed up flying frantically around the house. There were downy feathers all over the tatami, and spots of blood here and there too. Mii was attacking the struggling bird mercilessly, stopping briefly to enjoy watching it, then again going for it with her sharp claws. When I tried to pull her away she bared her fangs and hissed menacingly at me.

Another time there was a flock of wagtails surrounding the garden. Mii had brought back a chick that had fallen from its nest in the woods and was playing with it in the garden. The birds had heard it crying, and dozens of wagtails had gathered in trees near the house to threaten Mii, who kept her paw firmly on the chick, refusing to let it go.

By the time I managed to get her away from the

chick it was evening and already dark. My arms were all scratched up from where she had resisted.

Here in Shinagawa there was nothing of the springs and summers she had spent learning about the wild from other animals. There was no earth on the balcony, no shaded woods. Birds flew high overhead with no sign of ever coming down. There was no chance of suddenly coming up against a stray cat, or a seductive male tom. The only things crawling around were the small insects and spiders beneath the ornamental potted plants. Mii ignored these, and kept looking around in vain for real prey.

Not long after coming to Shinagawa she started waking me up in the middle of the night with her cries as she tried to find a way outside. She had probably started to miss the darkness once she started getting used to the new apartment and overcame her fear. She would go into the kitchen or sit in front of the metal door and wail incessantly. This wasn't like the mating calls of early spring, nor was it the way she miaowed when hungry. It was a deep, heavy voice coming from the centre of her body that I was hearing for the first time, a full-blooded primal cry of protest from the depths of her being.

In order to calm her down, in the quiet of the night when all the other residents were asleep, I opened the door to show her that there was nothing outside. In front of our apartment was the large elevator door, and the concrete box of the corridor enclosed by walls. There was nothing like grass or earth, no paths for her to follow.

Mii walked timidly along the fifth-floor concrete corridor, sniffing intently. She went to each identical door in turn, checking the smells, then moved on to the next one to sniff there for a while. Reaching the end of the corridor, she turned back with a look of utter bewilderment on her face. There were two external emergency staircases, and she stood on the landings not moving a muscle, frightened by the strange path leading up and down. Every time something touched the metal stairs there was a loud clang and she dashed back in a panic.

This teeny short night-time walk from the elevator to the ends of the corridor soon became an essential part of our routine. Even though she knew it didn't lead anywhere, having spent the day cooped up in the apartment it at least seemed to provide her with a little diversion.

Every day when I came home from work she would be waiting for me by the door and would give a little miaow, just as she had in Kokubunji. I would pick her up and as always she would lick my face then peep intently out into the corridor. Then she would go inside, eat her dinner, and later, when all the neighbours were asleep, she would come to my feet and pester me to let her out.

This gradually became her custom, and when she was ready for her walk I would have to join her regardless of whether I was working or needed to sleep. I would open the door for her and she would head up to the end of the corridor and back again. Once was not enough, though. She would come back with a dissatisfied look on her face as if to say, 'Is that it?', and head back out again. And she would often stop and prick her ears up listening for any presence inside the row of apartments before taking another step and twitching her nose to check for any new smells, so a walk of a mere twenty metres or so took a ridiculously long time.

Watching Mii fearfully, warily making her way up and down the corridor like a migratory fish, I crouched down by the door and told her over and over that it was okay. Nobody would come. It was the middle of the night, so even if someone did come along they weren't going to hurt her. I was here waiting with the door open, so there was no need to worry. She didn't need to be afraid.

After finishing her walk, Mii would come back into the apartment looking relieved, jump on to the chair and curl up. But she kept her ears perked up listening to the sounds from the streets outside, unable to sleep.

One autumn day when the wind was particularly strong, Mii was restless and listening intently to the laundry and the bamboo screens flapping about on the balcony.

She was remembering something. Missing something. Observing her out of the corner of my eye, I suddenly felt like crying. Maybe I should have left her in the familiar woods of Kokubunji, even if she did end up dying there. I listened to the autumn wind blowing in this urban district, still unable to fathom what it meant for an animal to be happy.

On the other hand, I couldn't help smiling at the thought of her going out into the corridor and me patiently waiting. Back in Kokubunji, Mii had been the one made to wait for me to come home. During the day she had killed time playing by herself, and at night she had waited devotedly for her human to return.

Now it was my turn to wait for her to come home every night. I wondered how she killed time during the day in our small apartment. I understood how she must feel with only her stuffed jaguar to play with, and at night I was willing to wait for her playtime to finish however long it took.

As winter approached, the swirling winds around our fifth-floor apartment grew stronger and we started hearing all sorts of new sounds. Other than the noise of traffic coming up from below, there was the rustling of the ginkgo trees on the side of the road, the sound of tin cans rolling along the street, and the electronic sounds of washing machines and kitchen appliances coming from other apartments, the sound of water running through drainpipes. Our first autumn in this apartment block stuffed full of the presence of people was coming to an end.

Rattle rattle the wind blows
Rattle rattle a lonely sound
Autumn comes in through every single hole
Making that sound

Is it reaching your ears too?
You crane your neck your eyes wander
Seeking out the winds of long ago
The nuts on the trees in the woods making you
  jump when they fall
And with the leaves, the smell of the earth

I want you to forget
We are in a new place now

Rattle rattle
I pick up the nuts fallen from the trees
Thinking of you playing on the floor at night
I pick up more and more my hands are full
Beech nuts jolcham acorns sweet oak acorns
Looking down as I walk along the road and through
  the park
Picking up fresh, sweet-smelling nuts

Then feeling melancholy
I look at the nuts I've just picked up
And throw them into the night current of the
  Meguro River

98

Mii Goes Missing

One year passed since coming to live here, then three years, and we were accustomed to our nightly walks in the corridor.

When Mii wanted to go out she would come to my feet and utter a brief *mi*. That was the signal for me to open the door for her. By then she was completely used to going out and knew that after one in the morning there were never any people in the corridor, so she jumped off her chair with a thud and came over to me.

When I was busy with my work I would open the door and let her play in the corridor on her own, but when I didn't have much to do I would go out with her and walk slowly along the deserted corridor.

Sometimes I would pick her up and take her down the emergency stairs to the car park below for a walk. On the ground floor there was a car park for residents, the cars all in rows. At first our walking route had taken in the small apartment gardens on the south side. When the flats were built, there must have been a lot of young couples for in one corner of the garden a small sandpit had been installed for children to play in, and it was planted with trees including cherry, hydrangea, fig and mikan orange. The caretaker looked after them well, for they always flowered every year.

On summer nights we would often walk around this garden. Being a coward, Mii would start shaking the moment I put her down on the unfamiliar ground and try to dash off, so I bought her a thin collar with a lead, and slowly walked with her at her own pace. She would take a step forward, listen alertly, then take another step and prick her ears up, just as she had done in the corridor.

Mii was miserable on these walks, utterly unable to relax. Sometimes she didn't move forward at all, and often she would freeze at the sound of a car passing on the other side of the wall. Even though there was a sandpit, she never went into it, only skirting around it. The street lamps beyond the wall were too bright, and she didn't seem to be able to relax without the deep darkness such as there had been in Musashino. Above her head there were numerous windows, and the presence of people inside them may have made her nervous too.

I soon stopped taking her into the garden. When I saw how fearful and tense she was, I no longer felt like taking a leisurely stroll. By the time we went back to the apartment, I myself was worn out from nerves. Instead, the car park behind the flats became the new place for our walks.

Unlike the garden, this was in the darkness behind the building. What's more, since it was set away from the road, the sound of traffic that Mii found so frightening was muffled. It was perfect, and all I had to do was carry her down the emergency stairs next to my flat that led straight to it. At first I put a collar and lead on her as I'd done in the garden, and walked slowly around with her.

There was one problem with this. Mii liked to explore under the cars, so the lead quickly got tangled up. Once I heard a *gya* and looked down to see her being choked by the lead tangled around her neck. Having learned my lesson, I removed her collar, and she started moving cautiously under the cars from one to another. She went quietly creeping around all the cars lined up in the silence.

Meanwhile, I sat on the emergency stairs and watched her, and when she took a long time to come back I would look under each car in turn to check where she was. She would usually hide under one car, sniffing the ground or play at stretching up under the car. Sometimes she came across a large stray cat that had made its territory under a car and hastily beat a retreat back to the emergency stairs. She was chased by this cat a number of times, and would dash up the stairs at top speed, slipping and losing her footing in her haste. But as she got used to going for walks here she became more confident, and no longer panicked when she came across the stray.

The stray also got used to this pet cat newcomer from upstairs, and they apparently felt a strong urge to check each other out for they stood stock-still staring curiously at each other from a distance as I watched patiently, fighting drowsiness. Then Mii would suddenly come back, the tension gone from her face, as though to say, 'That's enough for tonight.'

It didn't take long for Mii to start climbing the stairs on her own. Every time she came to a landing she would stop and look back at me clumping up the stairs in my shoes behind her.

Mii went on ahead and I followed behind; this was always how our walks went. Mii never once followed behind me, instead turning back frequently to check up on me.

But she didn't know where her own apartment was. All the landings were the same, all the curves were the same, and what's more all the emergency staircase doors and all the apartment doors were the same colour and shape, so unless I told her, 'Hey, we're home,' when we reached the fifth floor, she would keep on climbing up.

Our apartment must have smelled differently to the others, but ever since we'd moved here she had never been able to distinguish between the smells of the different floors and apartments.

And then one day it happened: Mii went missing. As always, I was sitting at my desk with the front door open. I had just bought a word processor, and I was absorbed in learning how to use it.

If anyone came along, she always came running back into the apartment at top speed. That night there was no sign of anything, and as far as I knew she was out playing in the corridor as always. She would sometimes sit on the landing of the emergency staircase and look intently down, but she never went down on her own. Maybe she was used to us going on walks together or maybe she was just too scared to go by herself, but she always stayed close to the apartment when she was left to play on her own. But that night when I suddenly went to check up on her, there was no sight of her anywhere in the corridor or on the stairs.

When Hyakken Uchida's cat Nora went missing, he went running around looking for it like a madman, tears streaming down his face and his nose running. He wrote all about it his book *Nora ya*, how people can even experience something akin to madness when they lose their cat. There was something ghastly about the vision of him thinking of his lost cat and burying his head in a cushion in agony, crying, 'Nora ya! Nora my love!', but I empathised with his distress. People didn't only feel affection for other humans, and I keenly understood Hyakken's pain when the cat he loved like a child went missing.

And like Hyakken, I too went weak at the knees. I sat in the entrance of my apartment the whole night, tears and snot streaming down my face, waiting for Mii to come home. I didn't just wait for her, I also searched every nook and cranny in the garden and the car park, and even ran out on to the highway outside, but morning came and I still hadn't found her.

I had read any number of tales of cats that had walked

over a hundred kilometres back to their old home, or who had been abandoned numerous times but always made their way home again, so it did occur to me to wonder whether Mii hated living in the apartment so much she had decided to try to find her way back to our old house, but she was such a scaredy-cat I couldn't believe she'd be able to cross the highway and make her way safely through the maze of city streets not even knowing east from west.

When the first pale rays of light appeared in the east, I still kept the apartment door open. I knew she wasn't in the flat, but I couldn't help searching inside the cupboard and the recesses of the bookcase over and over again. I had already lost all sense of reason. I had searched the car park multiple times. I had scrutinised both staircases all the way to the roof, and all the floors. I had searched inside the empty elevator numerous times to make sure she wasn't shut inside. I kept my ears peeled in case she was crying somewhere, but I couldn't hear her anywhere.

I sank down on to my haunches outside my apartment door as the sun rose and people started moving around. That morning everything was cast in a different light than usual.

Suddenly I had a vision of Mii suspended in mid-air stuck in a hole in the school fence all those years ago. Maybe she was dangling somewhere like that now, unable to make a sound? Or maybe she was stuck in some tiny space, struggling to free herself? Or of course she could also be flattened skin on a road somewhere, victim to a car.

After a while I heard the clomp clomp of someone running up the staircase. It was the newspaper delivery boy. The brisk sound of his sneakers bounding up the stairs grew closer to my floor, and stopped. Still with the bundle of newspapers under his arms, his eyes widened at the sight of me slumped on the floor. He seemed almost scared. I probably looked drunk, with my face all sticky with tears and snot and my hair a dishevelled mess. I had lost my senses, and just seeing his face made the tears well up again. I didn't care who he was, I just had to let someone know that Mii had disappeared.

'My cat's gone,' I told the boy in a muffled voice, waving my arms wildly. 'I've been waiting for her all night, but she hasn't come home . . .' I looked down and up, and all around. I couldn't find the words to explain it properly, and my hands kept moving up and down of their own will.

'Your cat? Ah . . .' the boy said in a strange voice, still looking bewildered. His voice hadn't come out strange because he was out of breath, rather it was his astonishment at having come across something so weird.

'You're going upstairs, aren't you? If you see a cat, be sure to tell me,' I told him. 'If you see a cat wandering around up there, she's mine. So do make sure you tell me, okay?' But he didn't come back. She wasn't anywhere to be found.

It was the caretaker M who finally told me where Mii was. I'd run into M that morning in the corridor when he came to do the cleaning, and told him the same thing I'd told the newspaper boy. Just before noon he received a call from a woman artist called N who lived upstairs. A cat had come into her flat last night so she was looking after it, but did he know whose cat it could be?

I felt profoundly stupid. And I also felt intensely angry. I had been looking for her all night and had even gone upstairs numerous times calling 'Mii' but she hadn't even answered me! At the same time, when I thought how upset I'd been the tears welled up again and I felt pathetic, and that made me want to cry again. I was in such a state that my tear glands were completely out of control.

My tear glands were still broken when N came down with Mii in her arms and said cheerfully, 'Oh, so she was from the floor right below me, then. She wasn't a stray after all!' My eyes and nose were streaming as I took Mii from her. I tried to ask Mii, 'What were you doing? Did you forget which apartment it was?' but all that came out of my throat was a sound like wind blowing through a broken shoji.

N looked amused. Chuckling, she stroked Mii's head and said lightly, 'She slept with me. She was such a good girl, you know.' She was trying to lighten the mood, I thought, and hugged Mii close to me, but Mii suddenly started to tremble violently. With her relief at finding her human, she too had lost all control and peed copiously all over me. She must have been holding it in all night.

Mii spent the whole day asleep. She didn't even miaow at the door that night either. She looked as though she had used up all her strength, and lay there energyless, like a molten lump of clay. She must have been playing on the emergency staircase and been unable to find her way home. And she had tried to catch my attention by miaowing, but she had been outside N's door instead of mine. N happened to like cats and had opened the door to let her in. And she had fed her, and cuddled her in bed. Then by the morning she had grown worried, and called the caretaker.

Mii looked out of it for a while after that. The next day N came again and teased her, 'Hey, kitty, surely you haven't forgotten me already?' And then added cheerfully, 'She trotted straight on in as if it were her own home and miaowed three times, you know.'

Meanwhile, Mii cowered with a hopeless look on her face, blinking. She looked absolutely pitiful, no doubt from the shock of having lost her way home. She didn't invite me out for our nightly walk for some time after that.

Thinking back, that was probably the onset of old age. Living in an apartment, her nose and legs were degenerating, and she had finally lost touch with the wild. Mii was stricken with that reality, and I was stricken by my own laziness at not having gone out for a walk with her that night.

And then six months or so later, Mii crawled into the tiny gap behind the toilet and stayed there, refusing to come out. She hardly ate, and only came out to relieve herself. I didn't know whether she was sick or whether she had withdrawn psychologically, but she stayed crouching there and made grumpy threatening sounds whenever I touched her. Her fur was dishevelled, and her face looked somehow stiff.

A vet who came on a house visit wondered whether it was her internal organs or bones, but in the end he couldn't say what was causing it. I had another veterinary clinic take an X-ray, but the cause remained unknown. Mii spent ten days behind the toilet like that, then one day she suddenly came out of the darkness, ate some food, and started walking slowly around the flat again. However, she was somehow different from before. I hadn't yet realised it, but Mii knew: old age was creeping up on her.

> *Cells die   so many, every day*
> *Countless deaths rear their heads*
> *The clear waters of today are no more*
>
> *I lie down and listen to your heartbeat*
> *Today a healthy tick tock   tock   tock*
> *But it is no longer   the sound of summer*

A FRESH START

The sound of autumn   the sound of winter
The sound of something going away

When I sleep   I can forget
The trees shedding their leaves   people who've gone
Food that is rotting and
Of course   the death of your cells
So   let's sleep
So as not to hear your departing footsteps

N and Hana

N painted really lovely pictures, watercolours and wood-block prints, all with exceptionally beautiful colours. Collages too, and oil paintings. She had continued to paint after leaving art school, she told me, specialising in book illustrations and covers. She had also studied art in New York, but due to poor health she'd moved back to Tokyo and was living quietly together with her mother.

After having met through Mii, we would often pay each other visits. We would sit and talk at the table in the simple, uncluttered kitchen of her bright south-facing flat upstairs. She liked rock music, and whenever I went to see her Rod Stewart was always playing loud. 'I only paint now and then. I get too tired,' she told me, little by little showing me her work from the past and more recent pieces. They were beautiful battlefields on paper that danced and bounded with colours overflow-ing, blending together, clashing with each other.

In-between talking about art, she would talk fast in a hoarse voice about how she liked New York best of all, and how she wanted to be an illustrator, not just paint pictures. Once, long ago, she kept a cat and a chicken together in the same apartment, she told me, laughing. 'They enjoyed frolicking in the air together. The chicken used to fly through the room, and the cat chased her. She really did spread her wings and fly! A flying chicken is really rare,' she said, holding her hand up to show how high the chicken flew, and gesticulating wildly as she told me about their noisy indoor antics.

I grew to like this eccentric artist, who was completely straightforward and unpretentious. She once showed me her belly squeezed into jeans with a too-tight waist, saying she'd grown fat and sad these days. She'd been slender and pretty way back when, she said, roaring with laughter. Sometimes she would visit me on a whim in the middle of the night when I was working in order to give me an apple newly arrived from her family in rural Niigata.

I also remember her saying, 'Colours are strong. I love colours. They have music to them.' When she learned that I used to write poetry, she commented, 'Words trump painting. I hate poets, cos I can never outdo them.'

She would intersperse a few tasteful lines of text alongside her art. These were extravagant, mescaline-tinged pieces by the likes of Henri Michaux; glossy, exhil-arating words that were strangely captivating.

We would meet in either my place or hers in the quiet of the night when everyone else was asleep.

Whenever N came to mine, she would always rub

Mii's ears or stroke her chin and say invitingly, 'Kitty-chan, how come you never visit me any more? Come on over! Let's sleep together again!' but Mii just turned away, having learned her lesson. In fact, when N came over Mii always looked miserable. She remembered it well, that night. That thought made me feel miserable too, and the two of us would sit hanging our heads.

When N was in her own apartment listening to Rod Stewart, she would be in a good mood and talk about how she would love to have another cat, or how she wanted to go to New York again, and her travel plans.

'Oh, I want to fall in love!' she shouted. 'Being in love is wonderful. I haven't been in love for months. I would be if I were in New York, though!' 'I haven't been in love for years!' I shouted back. 'But I want to fall in love in Tokyo, not New York!' Those were innocent, carefree times between women. We would talk non-stop, like late-night radio.

I'd known her for over a year when she suddenly said, 'A beautiful white cat was dumped downstairs.'

It was true, every night when I came home from work, I saw a pure white cat peeping out from the bushes to the south of the garden, or from the shadows of the automatic vending machine. She had a gentle, round face, and was friendly with people. When I held my hand out, she unhesitatingly rubbed her face against it. Seeing her eyes look questioningly at people's faces, I knew she must have been a well-loved pet. I didn't know how long she had been there, but according to N somebody who had lived in these flats had abandoned her when they moved. And the cat had stayed, always waiting by the entrance for her human to come back.

'I mean, as soon as she hears footsteps, she comes running. But then she immediately looks disappointed. She must have thought I was her human. I feed her sometimes.'

It was against the building rules to give food to stray cats. There were notices in the caretaker's handwriting: 'Please do not feed the cats.' I don't know who gave the cat a name, but at some point she had come to be known as Hana. Several people were feeding her. One night I went down to check on her, suddenly feeling worried, only to find pet food put out diffidently on a styrofoam tray. The next night and the night after that, food was put out for her without fail.

N was one of those. And H on the top floor. Before I knew it I had joined them, forming a small allied army for Hana. Nobody said openly that they were feeding her, but when I went down to put out my rubbish, I realised that more than a few people were looking out for her.

Hana was a very faithful cat. Her owner must have abandoned her due to circumstances, but Hana was always in the same place where they had left her, waiting for them to come back, never doubting that they would. Whenever she heard footsteps, she would come out of the bushes to check people's faces, and if you called her she would always poke her trusting white face out and run up to you.

That friendliness made life difficult for her. She never once showed any aggression whatsoever either to people or to any of the stray cats roaming the area. Her gentle, utterly unguarded nature meant that she was often targeted by the strays. She didn't resist, so would always end up with a scratched nose or her back would be all sooty from having been chased into a tight corner.

Whenever I came across one of the allied army, we would often say how awful it was of her owner to have abandoned her like that, but nobody knew who it was or which flat they had lived in.

That was often the case with apartment buildings. Even though we all lived in the same place behind the building's steel front entrance, we rarely had anything to do with each other, and even I had no idea of who lived on other floors. When I came across other people in the entrance hall, I often didn't know whether they were residents or visitors.

Yet judging by the way Hana always stayed in the same place, I knew she must have belonged to someone who had lived here.

Then one night, it was past one o'clock in the morning when I finished working, and to clear my head I took my rubbish downstairs to the collection area. It was a really cold night. I caught sight of a couple crouching down next to the bushes where Hana always hid. The young man and woman were wearing thick coats and were stroking Hana. The woman's face was hidden by the hood of her coat, but her cheeks looked sickly. When they saw me, they stopped stroking Hana and said, 'Good evening.'

The woman's voice sounded like her nose was blocked. It suddenly hit me. This couple must be Hana's owners. They had abandoned her, but it was so cold tonight that they had been worried and come to check on her. 'That cat was abandoned, you know,' I said tentatively. 'She's such a good girl, always here waiting for her owner to come back. She's very sweet, so some of us cat lovers here have been looking after her.'

Neither of them said anything. I had the feeling a look passed briefly between them, but it might just have been my imagination. Since they still didn't answer, I took the elevator back up to my apartment, but it was on my mind so before going to sleep I went back down, but the young couple had already gone. Hana was curled up on the cold earth alone, a dejected look on her face. Maybe that couple hadn't been her humans after all? Or maybe they had? I couldn't know which. But if they were, maybe they'd come to apologise to her and explain why they couldn't keep her.

This brought a lump to my throat, as I recalled walking around trying to find a place where I could live with Mii. Even when you were desperate to keep your cat, sometimes you had no choice but to abandon it however much it hurt. If I hadn't managed to find a place for us to live,

Mii too would probably have ended up in the woods in Kokubunji waiting for her human to come back, just like Hana.

Not long after that, Hana was badly injured, with a split ear and numerous gashes all over her body. She had been attacked by a stray. She was always being targeted, but this time the wounds were really terrible. H was the one to take her to the vet.

After that, Hana became H's cat and went to live in H's eleventh-floor apartment with a large rooftop balcony. There she basked in the sun, never to be chased by people or stray cats again.

Every time I thought of Hana, I would look up to the top of the tall apartment block. Having stayed curled up on the earth waiting for her owner to come back, Hana had at last found a new home. I would feel a prickle at the back of my nose whenever I thought of her having a warm place to sleep, and her gentle white face being hugged close by H. And with her new family, she had a new name, Shiro. Now she was living a new life as Shiro, playing happily bathed in light.

But not long afterwards N, Mii's only friend, disappeared. She died unexpectedly, out of the blue. I didn't know exactly how old she was, but I will always remember her round face and husky voice, and the shape of her well-built hips and youthful thighs enclosed in jeans.

I had a number of her paintings in my apartment, which she had given me as gifts. One was a colourful collage that seemed to pulse, like Rod Stewart's music. Another looked like a self-portrait, the face of a woman. This face was enshrined at the centre of my bookcase, the face she'd had when she teased Mii, 'Kitty-chan, how come you never visit me any more? Come on over! Let's sleep together again!'

I stood dazed on the emergency staircase where I had sometimes sat with her. Hana was at the top of the building where my deceased friend had lived, and below her, the apartment where my friend should have been was empty. And even now, some nights I had the feeling I could hear N's nasal voice calling, 'Kitty-chan, Kitty-chan!'

4

Into the Twilight

Urine Everywhere

We animals start off as small balls. We come into existence as a round nucleus in our mother's womb, where we
are enveloped in warm fluid as our hands and feet and
bones and bumps of flesh take shape. We come into the
world in our various forms, as cats, as dogs, as humans.
Then comes the time when we slowly fall apart. How fast
that happens . . .

In 1993, I recognised the signs of it starting in my cat.

Her urine was pale pink. How long had it been stained
that colour? It didn't show up so well in her toilet litter,
but there were spots of pink on the mats in the kitchen
and bathroom.

It was the smell that alerted me to the fact that something was wrong. It was clearly coming from somewhere
other than her toilet, which I kept by the bathroom door.
Looking around the apartment, I was dumbfounded.
There were traces of incontinence all over the cork tiles
I'd put down in place of the old vinyl flooring. Some were
blackish stains, others still glistening.

I investigated further and found with a heavy heart

that the cover of Mii's favourite chair was also speckled with stains indicating she had been incontinent for several days.

That wasn't all. A strong smell was also coming from under the chair below the north-facing window. There were traces of bloodstained urine everywhere Mii would walk, all her favourite places.

For the past week I had been cleaning her toilet and changing the litter more often because I'd had the feeling it smelled more than usual, but it hadn't been coming from there after all. It had been emanating throughout the apartment from where her urine had soaked into the floor.

For the past year, I had frequently rushed Mii to a vet clinic on the National Highway when her haunches had given away and she had been unable to walk. They had taken X-rays, but nothing was wrong with her bones. Blood tests had shown no sign of infection. Stumped, the vet had prescribed vitamins and painkillers, and whether those had worked or for some other reason, Mii had started walking again with no further ado.

The symptoms kept coming back to a greater or lesser degree, but she didn't seem to be in pain, and she was eating well.

Mii had suddenly started putting on weight around 1990, and she had grown so fat the vet had warned me to be careful. Her weight had increased from around 3 kilograms to 5 kilograms, and she looked plump and heavy walking around the apartment. He kept recommending that I feed her diet food, but she just turned her nose up at it whenever I tried.

What she liked was grilled horse mackerel and sardines, and dried bonito stewed in a sweet sauce. And she gobbled up dried bonito flakes and small dried sardines. With unhealthy eating habits like these, it wasn't surprising that she had put a burden on her internal organs. But when I noticed the blood in her urine and rushed her back to the vet, there was nothing wrong with her kidneys, nor any sign of a tumour in her stomach.

The only tests left were for the bladder and urinary tract, but I didn't want to put her through the pain of an endoscope. The vet agreed, and told me that there probably was something there but even if he successfully operated on her there was no guarantee that she would recover.

Mii was already at an age when any deterioration in her health would not be surprising.

Cats don't get wrinkled faces or stooped backs like humans do. Their bodies still look young and their fur retains its colour, and Mii even still had all her teeth. Her urine was tinged with blood but the amount was normal, she didn't appear to be in pain, and she was eating well. The vet told me that if she continued to have blood in her urine for a long time, then we would consider what to do about it, but strangely enough, it stopped for a while afterwards. Just like before, when she had spent about ten days crouching in the dark behind the toilet and her symptoms had cleared up on their own, this time too she recovered and the blood disappeared.

I kept telling myself that I was used to these repeated episodes that humans couldn't explain, but of course it still came as a shock every time I saw blood in her urine.

Some nights, before going to sleep, I couldn't help holding my hand under Mii's bottom to check for drips of urine, and some mornings the first thing I did was to run my eyes over every corner of the flat where Mii had been and hastily grab a dishcloth. If she was dripping red blood, I rushed her back to the clinic. Every time I put her into the carrier, she would wail loudly.

Yet every time I took her to the vet, the result was always the same. They couldn't tell what was wrong with her. Meanwhile, it was just stressing Mii out. Whenever she saw the carrier on the floor, her fear of the vet came back to her and she crawled behind the futon in the cupboard and there was no budging her. Whenever I tried to give her medicine, too, she would run away and growl menacingly if I got too close. When I did manage to pin her down and force the medicine down her throat, I would be overcome by an unspeakable sense of guilt. But for those of us who own pets, we are the only ones who can walk with them as they age.

I stroked her now soft, fat body all over, and combed her fur, which had started falling out, and bought a lot of new mats to cover the stains on the floor from her bloody urine. I started keeping my eyes out for soft fabrics. There was a pile of offcuts for use in quilting on a trolley outside a store for Western dressmaking fabrics, and I bought a number of those and stitched them together with my sewing machine to make mats.

I put these mats on Mii's favourite chair, inside her cardboard-box house, on top of pee pads I'd found in the market. All I had to do to clean up after her was to wash them, and every evening there was the sound of my washing machine at work on my balcony, and the sight of the colourful mats hung up to dry on the clothes pole outside and in the bathroom.

While Mii's condition and mood fluctuated daily, the fact that I didn't suffer at all might have been because I was dealing with an animal. Being a cat, she couldn't use words to complain of pain, or suffering, or displeasure, and she looked absolutely innocent as she watched her human labour over the washing every night. Whenever I saw that innocent face, the tension would leave me. Her earnest, vaguely reassured expression as she watched people: that was this cat's virtue. She never frowned, never pouted. Her unquestioning gaze somehow managed to stir my exhausted heart.

Before going to bed I was now checking Mii's bottom, amount of earwax, the colour and lustre of her paw beans, eyes, hip bones, urine, faeces, and so forth. I inspected everything, the amount of food she ate, the amount of water she drank. I didn't know how long she had left, but I knew she was nearing the end. I had begun to think that being prepared would come from concrete things like the daily quantities of urine and how much food she ate rather than anything abstract.

As well as carefully observing her, I recalled the vet telling me that the biggest worry was that her muscles would weaken and she would spend all her time sleeping, so I made sure that we never missed our nightly walk, at least.

We had long stopped going downstairs to the car park. Mii wasn't able to walk very far any more, and if I accompanied her she would take a few steps then sink down on the floor. She would just wait silently until I went to get her, as long as it took. I didn't know whether her legs and haunches had grown weak after she started putting on weight, or whether they had weakened and she had put on weight because it was difficult to move. Our walking route had been reduced to the fifth-floor corridor and one or two storeys up and down the staircase, and it took considerably less time than it used to.

Despite Mii's reluctance, I would pat her back and tell her to walk. Together we would walk and walk, and stay alive, I told her. I didn't know how far a cat should walk every day to stay healthy, but a cat confined to an apartment all day must need a certain amount of exercise.

So, we walked. I would make the most of any spare moment in the night to take her for lots of short outings.

Beneath the pale flickering fluorescent lights of the corridor and the stairs, and another night on the cold, rain-swept emergency stairs. As long as we kept doing this, she could continue to live, I kept repeating to the both of us.

The blood in Mii's urine appeared intermittently, but I would look at her soft fat body and tell myself that she was still okay.

Animals were natural creatures to begin with. They had much better natural healing powers than humans, but you could never avoid death whatever you did. I didn't know how much longer Mii would live, but I wanted to spend as much time with her as I could, doing fun things with as little suffering as possible.

The apartment stank of urine, but as long as Mii wasn't in pain I didn't care. When she was well, she would lie on her back in puddles of sunlight, belly up, with a peaceful look on her face. When she was lying with her legs sticking up, letting her belly receive the full rays of sun from the east, I would call her and she would just turn her head to look at me and give a contented *nya*. Sometimes she wouldn't say anything, just move her mouth in a smile.

I would smile wryly and tell her I didn't have a clue what was wrong with her. When she was lying down I would lie on my tummy next to her, reading a book. Our apartment was small, but there was also the happiness of knowing we were safe and secure here.

There were times when Mii would gaze fixedly at me without moving a muscle. When I saw her face like that, I remembered with a pang the pain I'd felt at losing her, even though it had been just for one night.

I'd seen myself clearly then. How distraught I'd been when she disappeared. That occasion had brought home to me that I could never walk away from this relationship. We would be together until the end. I think it was when Mii peed in my arms that I saw how we mutually supported each other.

At the same time, my mind filled with wonder at how I'd once thought it might be better to leave Mii behind in Kokubunji, and how I'd left my husband but not her.

I could no longer part with her. If that parting was to come, this time it wouldn't be that she'd gone missing, it would be a different kind of parting. There were probably no words for it. A silent farewell.

And with this knowledge, I could no longer look down on Mii from above. I had to get down low, quietly peering with her into the world as she saw it.

> *For some time now   a small boat has been*
> *   floating   through my nights*
>
> *I put my cat in a boat   in the river's flow*
> *Searching for her   I call her name*
> *Mii   where is it taking you now?*

I want you to sing   so I can know where you are
I want you to cry   so I can see you as you were here

The boat in my dreams is round
Like a womb   warm and soft

My cat is being carried away   becoming smaller
*   and smaller*
Soft, fine fur reaches me on the breeze
Oh, I have to go and bring her back
She shouldn't be on the boat alone
The voice of my cat   no longer able to return
*   whirling in the wind*

I've had this dream so many times

The Pet Sitter

One of the big problems facing anyone with a pet is what to do when you are away from home. Ideally a family member can stay behind and care for them, but for those who live alone or who travel a lot for work it is a constant source of worry. Of course there are different types of pets, and some cats are free to come and go outside while others are indoor only. One of my friends said that when he had to go away for work, he always left a window open so his cat could come and go. He lived in a ground-floor flat with a garden which, although small, his cat could access through the window. When he went away, he left several days' worth of food and water inside the flat. The cat was used to going to the toilet in the garden, so that wasn't an issue. He never had to worry about his cat, although he was of course still concerned about how his cat was doing while he was away.

I lived on the fifth floor, so this was not an option for me. Leaving a window open was not a problem, but the toilet needed cleaning, and I could never relax once

I started worrying about whether she'd spilt the water or had run out of food, so I couldn't go away for long.

When I absolutely had to go away, I would get a friend who liked cats to look after her. But while this was fine for a day, I felt bad about getting her to come every day when I was away for three or four days.

One time I had to go to my mother's place for a few days, so I put Mii in the carrier and took her with me. But that trip turned out to be stressful and exhausting for both of us. It was more tiring than I'd expected to carry Mii, who now weighed 5 kilograms, from the Shinkansen to a local train station, and then getting around by taxi. And I was constantly on edge in case she cried on the train or wet herself.

If she were used to travelling it would be one thing, but Mii was so timid it took a lot of coaxing just to get her to the neighbourhood vet clinic.

And she once ran away from me when we were at my mother's. We were just about to go back to Tokyo and I was putting her into the carrier when she suddenly bit my hand and hid in the dark. She must have thought I was taking her to yet another unfamiliar place, or worse, that I was going to abandon her. She kept running from one hiding place to another, and it wasn't easy to catch her. Luckily it was in my mother's house, but just the thought of her running away anywhere else was enough to send a chill down my back.

Then one day I was glancing through a newspaper and gasped when I came across a story about a pet sitter, Y, who later became my saviour.

Y had originally worked as an English teacher in a cram school and an office assistant in a translation agency. One day she had been unable to take her pet cat to the vet because she had to go to work, and this had prompted her to start a pet-sitting service that catered to single women, old people who were no longer able to take their beloved dogs out for walks and people wanting to travel abroad, taking over care of their pets, walking their dogs, and so on. By then she had some one hundred clients. A photo of her showed a beautiful woman with gentle features who really looked as though animals would love her.

I cut the article out and put it in my bag, thinking I would need to call on her services sometime, and had been carrying it around ever since.

Just as I had thought, it wasn't long before I had to make an SOS call to her. Some work had come up that meant I absolutely had to go to Kyushu for two or three nights, and the friend who usually helped me wasn't available.

I was amused to find that she started by interviewing me. Y was as she had appeared in her photo, a soft and gentle person with intelligent eyes. First she stroked Mii's head and greeted her, 'Mii-chan, what a good girl you are,' then without further ado primly took a seat and produced some white paper and a pen out of her bag. The paper turned out to be a client record, which she spread out on the table and went through the questions with me.

'What kind of food does Mii-chan like? What are her favourite toys? Is there anything wrong with her health? Is there a local vet clinic that she attends? What is the contact number for emergencies?'

Other questions included whether Mii went for walks or not, what sort of personality she had, and if there was anything she disliked. Y even took into consideration her clients' privacy, asking if there were any rooms she shouldn't enter. She noted down each answer on the record in soft, rounded handwriting.

I didn't know much about the pet industry. I went to pet shops, but it was hard to know from the outside how much the owners or employees actually knew about animals.

But Y seemed a lot more knowledgeable than the usual pet shop assistants, at least for dogs and cats. There was something in her quiet, clear voice that made me think this. Also her method was to care for the pet in the same way as their owners normally did as much as possible, and to adapt to the pet's own personality and habits. The purpose of the interview, therefore, was to learn about their normal lifestyle.

She seemed to understand the best and least stressful way to connect with animals. I had previously gone to see a pet hotel just in case the need arose, but my heart sank when I saw the dogs and cats shut in small cages waiting for their owners to return. It was far better for them to remain in their familiar home with as little change as possible to their daily routine, and to adapt the care to the animal's own needs, not just following a human's one-sided manual.

As I listened to Y, I watched the way she stroked Mii as she talked, impressed. Mii was lying relaxed, her face utterly at ease as Y slowly caressed her, searching for the spots that felt good. I could see the movements of her hand showed a natural thoughtfulness of someone who was used to animals. White hands. Hands that had a gentle rhythm. The movement of hands tuning in to the animal. It was hypnotic, like hand magic.

I came home from Kyushu to find a log sheet neatly filled in with Mii's data for each day placed on my desk. How much food she had eaten, her pee and poop history, and even how much she had played and how. Y had written it all down.

'When I opened the door, Mii-chan miaowed and came running, but when she saw it wasn't her owner she looked miffed and retreated into her box. She seemed a little happier when I stroked her, and after a while she fell asleep.'

I smiled as I read this. Mii evidently hadn't given Y a friendly welcome. The log sheet communicated very clearly how Mii and Y had interacted.

Y took care of Mii many times after that. Just knowing that she would be going to see her every day was enough to put me at ease while on a trip. The log sheet from Y was always there when I got home. I looked forward to seeing those, too. Reading it, I could see that Mii had had stomach problems, or that she had been in an exceptionally good mood.

Having come to know Y had taken a big load off my shoulders with regards to Mii, but unfortunately our relationship didn't last very long as Mii's condition noticeably worsened. I was no longer comfortable with leaving her, and couldn't ask either my friend or Y to care for her any more. Mii's old age had progressed to the point that she began to need nursing care that only her human could give her.

Using My Hands

It was in the early 1990s that her legs began to decline. Her haunches would suddenly give way while she was walking around the apartment. Unable to stand, she would remain with her bottom on the floor and move by dragging her body along. When this happened, she couldn't use her toilet properly any more, and would slip and fall bottom first into it.

Every time she did this, she would get covered in urine, and wet litter would scatter around the room. What's more, she started dripping urine constantly. This meant the whole apartment stank so strongly that it was suffocating.

I wondered whether she had hurt her back or legs jumping up on to a chair or walking out in the corridor without my realising. When her haunches had given way before she'd had blood in her urine, but this time there was no blood, just she would suddenly lose all strength in her legs. It started happening more and more frequently, and sometimes I'd even come home from work to find her collapsed in a sea of urine, her front legs waving about as she struggled. The moment I opened the door and came in, she would let out a shrill wail as though annoyed with herself.

This gradually started to happen more often, until eventually I took her to the vet for the first time in ages. I wanted to know if there was anything wrong with her leg bones or back, but the cause lay elsewhere. Her condition was far more serious than that.

'Her intestines have given up the ghost,' the vet said. 'They've lost their elasticity, like an old rubber band.' With old age, her intestines' peristaltic movement had weakened, and she was no longer able to defecate on her own. The reason she suddenly became unable to walk was that a large number of stools were stuck in her intestine, and the burden of that affected her back.

I gaped at him. 'Intestines? Stools?'

But it was no laughing matter. My cat was now dying of a faecal blockage.

Mii had only been pooping a small amount of hard stools every day for some time. I had noticed this, but it had never occurred to me that there could possibly be more accumulating inside her body. She had probably been straining to get them out, but her intestines had just not cooperated. Then the vet pointed out a chain of balls on the X-ray and said something horrifying: many cats and dogs had died because of being unable to eliminate faeces.

'It's usually due to ageing internal organs. The stools get as hard as cement, and when that happens it's really difficult to get it out. I've had to operate on dogs to get it out before now. It's all very well if you know what the problem is, but there are cases where a dog has died without my knowing why and I've only found out when conducting an autopsy. Even if you do manage to get them out, the intestines themselves have lost their function and the body has been weakened, so it's always going to be a problem.'

Dying of poop sounded kind of funny, but it was too miserable. Seeing the string of balls in the X-ray, I had to ask the vet bluntly if it was possible to get them all out. Generally speaking, the only way to get them out would be to force her to excrete them, he said. That would take time, so I should go home for now. He would do whatever he could.

He called back that evening, and on my way home from work I dropped into the clinic to find Mii in a cage hooked up to a drip, looking exhausted. She had been given numerous doses of medicine to soften the stools, as well as an enema. When I looked at her belly, I saw that where it had been so hard and distended was now totally flat. I had made a terrible mistake: I'd thought that she was so plump and round from eating so much, but that hadn't been the case at all.

I picked her up in my arms. Her body gave off an awful stench of disinfectant mixed with excrement. This was the smell of old age. The smell of the hopeless decline of her organs.

That evening, I sat for a long time with Mii in the bath, washing her. Tears welled up in my eyes as I slathered her with human shampoo smelling of roses and held her in my arms, lifting her up and down in the warm water. Inside this soft body, there were parts that were no longer able to fulfil their function properly. The tubes that eliminated waste were no longer tubes, having become limp like old rubber bands. Her body so full of energy, like a spring mechanism, had started dying inside. The collapse of life had started quietly out of sight.

For the longest time I sat gently swaying Mii in the warm water. I placed her, covered in a sweet smell, on my knees swaying her soft body, and when the water started to get cold I added more hot water. Watching the white fur on her now-empty belly part and close, I could see that it was not just her intestines that were slowly declining, but the spring in her legs too.

The next day, Mii ate up her breakfast as if nothing had happened, but her symptoms became a regular cycle and every two months I had to take her to the clinic. When her intestines started to be blocked, first of all there would be pressure on her bladder and she would start to continually drip urine. Then her haunches would give way and she would start dragging herself around the floor.

When it reached this point, I had to throw up my hands. Mii would have to receive the same treatment as before, but her intestines themselves would never recover and it would keep happening again and again. Over time she gradually lost the ability to defecate on her own, and it was clear that she was growing weaker and weaker.

After having taken her to the clinic numerous times, I got the vet to prescribe her an oral medication to stimulate her bowel movements. It was a Chinese herbal medicine that looked like ground black sesame seeds. I would scoop some up with an earpick and put it into capsules to be administered morning and evening.

At first I got the transparent capsules from the vet, but once I discovered I could buy them at the neighbourhood pharmacy I would go to buy new capsules at the end of every month. To begin with I bought the same size as the ones I had received from the vet, but after a few months I switched to the next size up, checking with my own eyes and hands whether the medicine was still effective or not.

If she obediently took the medicine, she would be okay tomorrow, and the next day and the day after that. Her bowels would move. I wanted to believe this. Every evening, I stuffed the medicine into the shiny capsule. Before going to sleep I would shove it into her mouth and gently rub her belly.

That day too I had given Mii her medicine, and was rubbing her white belly as she lay there. It was beginning to swell again, and there appeared to be quite a lot of stools stuck inside. Suddenly, as I slid my hand lower down her belly, I touched something round and hard.

It was her bladder, swollen from the pressure from her intestines. I casually pressed it and nearly jumped out of my skin. Urine spurted straight up out of it. It had been accumulating in there, and every time I pressed it the shiny liquid gushed out on to the floor.

It was coming out! The tightly distended sac shrank each time I pressed it. Mii let me do it. She narrowed her eyes as though it felt good, and then she got up by herself and shook her back.

Thereafter, every morning and night I would feel Mii's lower belly with my hand. If it was distended I would take her to the toilet and press it. We crouched by the toilet and watched the warm golden liquid gush out until the sac was empty. This was a newly discovered 'prescription for life'. Every time she drank from the water bowl next to her food, our ritual was repeated.

Then, a few mornings later, after releasing her urine as usual, I was rubbing her belly and felt a number of hard, round objects, and knew they were lumps of faeces. Lots of balls were beginning to accumulate in her belly again. I pressed a little harder, and tried pushing them towards her anus. Little by little, the balls moved through her intestine. It was just like pushing balls through a pliant tube towards the exit. And then a small ball fell out on to the litter with a plop.

'Oh, a poop!' I exclaimed out loud. And as I kept pushing, out popped another, and then another, as Mii planted her feet firmly and strained. So I could get her poop out too! With a little help, Mii's body was functioning.

It was all by hand. Using my hands was effective.

I was glad I no longer had to rely on the vet or the clinic. There wasn't any need to face the physically demanding treatment with dread or to worry too much about it. I only had to touch her belly to know how much urine had accumulated, and if her haunches became unsteady and her legs got shaky, all I had to do was to lend her a hand with pushing it all out.

Once Mii's insides had been relieved, she walked unbelievably well. For a while she even started playing with her forgotten jaguar toy. She dragged it all around the apartment, miaowing cheerfully as if chattering away, and then slept with a cherubic face. Sometimes she would carry the jaguar by its tail, and sometimes just stand there with it still in her mouth, looking vacant. It was ages since I had seen this face, at peace and tired of playing.

I had never been so happy with the work of my own hands. How useful they were! Although of course I had to wash them thoroughly afterwards . . .

Mii was already over fifteen years old. How old would that be in human terms? Seventy or eighty? I didn't know if fifteen years was a long life for a cat or not, but all I knew from the state of her bowels and the evident weakness in her haunches was that she didn't have all that much time left.

Just one year, or two, or maybe three. I wanted to

spend that time with the two of us living quietly together. I wanted to spend every day using my hands two, three or even four times to help her. Stuffing medicine into capsules. Breaking up stewed bonito, boiling finely chopped meat.

When she was little, she had always jumped up on to the table while my husband and I were having dinner, wanting to taste a bit of everything that we were having. She would snatch a bit of instant ramen and run off with it in her mouth, or seem to want a whole piece of grilled mackerel in her own bowl. Her food preferences constantly came and went between cat food and human food, and she would happily eat most things other than glass noodles or konnyaku strips.

As she gradually aged, her taste in food also changed, and rather than soup stock or pet food she began to like lightly sweetened cooked food. She preferred stewed bonito, rather than raw. Grilled sardines, rather than raw. She had apparently grown disgusted by the smell of raw food. With meat, too, she liked the non-fatty part parboiled.

While putting effort into preparing foods like this for her, I would also take her on to my knees and remove the earwax that had been building up lately. Every time I approached her holding a cotton bud, she would gently lick and nibble my hand as if welcoming it. How good her ears must have felt! The wax that was so itchy and ticklish had gone.

Running my hands all over Mii's body, I felt an intimacy we had never had when she was young running from her body to mine, and from my body to hers, supporting each other.

An imaginary conversation with my cat-loving friends

How old is she?   *She's fifteen now*
Her colour, look!   *A white and black and brown calico, as you can see*
Her sweet voice
Her face   *Like a sweet baby*
She's so well behaved   *And a scaredy-cat*
Will you hold her?
You are my friend, so please do

Her name is Mii
Her first cry became her name
And she has made that same cry ever since

Come and hear that cry!
Before this child dies
While there is still a shine to her voice
Sincerely yours

A Neighbourhood Transforming

I wonder what on earth is buried here in the reclaimed land. The first time I walked here, the same question rose up like mist in my mind. The area between the sea and the old Tokaido highway where it runs from Yatsu-yamabashi down through Kita Shinagawa to Minami Shinagawa is entirely reclaimed land. Starting in the Edo period, slowly over time, land to live on was extended further and further into the sea.

I can't quite recall when development started on the area, but one day I noticed the shadow of a steel frame looming over the sea and it spread day by day as construction got under way on the new neighbourhood of Tennozu. When I first came here, it was a vast, barren wasteland. Huge warehouses lined the roads almost as far as the Shinagawa wharf, and the canal banks were occupied by concrete and transport companies. Along the bayshore road, all you could see here and there was the fence enclosing the wasteland inside which trailers and large trucks were constantly moving around. The ground in this wasteland was still uneven, and it was densely covered in goldenrod.

I would make my way through this inorganic landscape, passing from canal to canal along the banks. Once I reached the thermal power station near the undersea tunnel leading to Odaiba, there was hardly a soul in sight. It was just like being in a desert. But I liked this walk, it made me feel like an animal in the wilderness.

Inside the fence was a vast rubbish dump full of empty cans and soft drinks bottles, fluttering paper and plastic bags thrown out by the drivers of the trailers and trucks.

On fine days I would head out aimlessly to the reclaimed land. I would go to the wharfs and absently watch a large tanker docking then go back home, or catch my breath at the beauty of the sky visible between the containers. The contrast between the rust colour and the blue sky was eerily beautiful.

That inorganic landscape had changed before my very eyes, and the wilderness was long gone. Tennozu was by now a popular dating spot for young couples, and the expanse of land on the canal banks where before there was nothing had now been covered in smart boardwalks. The walls of hotels and apartment blocks glittered against the clear blue sky as the light bounced off them.

Every time I saw it, it felt like being in a dream. I couldn't for the life of me believe how this neighbourhood, which I knew nothing about when I first set foot in it and fell in love with the now-vanished wilderness, could have changed so much over so few years.

And it wasn't only Tennozu. The area around Osaki Station a mere ten-minute walk from my place had been washed away by a huge wave of development. The smell of welding, the blue light, the raw tang of rusting iron and steel emanating from the small neighbourhood factories. An excruciatingly humble area where the form of manual labour was in your face. It was all covered by a swarm of large buildings, strangely just as my cat was beginning to get old.

As I walked through the neighbourhood, I couldn't help thinking how much my own life had transformed over the years since I first moved here trying to convince myself that things would somehow work out.

The most important part of this transformation was that I had grown accustomed to living alone with Mii, and to the editorial production work I had started with the woman who gave me a job, and to other friends, and the things I had been writing not knowing whether they would ever come to anything had now taken on a life of their own. Before I knew it, I had become an established writer.

As the long, long years passed, I was crawling out of a dark tunnel. The days I had spent without knowing what I wanted to write had nurtured me without my realising it.

It had all started with a kitten. Without Mii, I

would never have come to live in this neighbourhood. I would never have wandered around every nook and cranny of the reclaimed land, or gazed upon the seasonal colours of the water in the network of canals. Nor would I have become so absorbed in listening to the embryo of a neighbourhood transforming.

The reason I could pinpoint so many achievements in the years that had passed was that I hadn't actually been alone. I hadn't been able to live with another person, but living with Mii I had become sensitive to the smell and the presence of the breeze over the seasons, the warmth of the light. After Mii had started getting old and infirm and I had established a regular routine of the hours I spent working and the times I went to bed and got up, I became even more sensitive to the sounds around me and the changes in the body of the animal I lived with.

When Mii was fast asleep, I would walk quietly around the apartment. As she stopped liking the hard dry food she had in the past and favoured softer, soupy food, the sound of her crunching on her food became less and less frequent, and eventually there was only the sound of her quietly lapping up wet foods like raw egg and milk.

In early spring I would take breaks in my nightly work to go down to an empty plot on the narrow street to look for the weeds that Mii liked. I didn't know much about weed types, but I knew which ones she did and didn't like.

In the years since moving here and making my cat the centre of my life, I realised that my time with Mii hadn't been disturbed even for a moment. While I'd struggled with breaking up with my husband, being forced out of my job, and several relationships with people that hadn't gone well, there wasn't a single thing that I'd ever felt had been lost between Mii and myself.

Mii had always been there. Even when I'd been working or spending time with friends, whether she was self-aware or not, she had remained at my side, her demeanour and expression unchanged as she aged. According to de Beauvoir, 'You do not die from being born, nor from having lived, nor from old age. You die from something. (. . .) Nothing that happens to a man is ever natural,' and it was the same for animals, wasn't it? They died in accidents, of illnesses, or were killed. But my cat was different. At least the Mii before me was ageing, just like a neighbourhood changing slowly at an imperceptible speed.

I no longer listened to music. Mii spent a lot of time sleeping and I didn't want to disturb her peaceful rest.

Here in this apartment, where the summer breeze passed through from the east to the north and in autumn and winter from the north to the east, I listened to the sounds of the constantly changing neighbourhood while also thinking of the death that would soon come to Mii.

It was definitely coming. It was already close by. Amid the smell of her body waste that never went away however much I cleaned, and the not-so-short time spent on emptying her bladder and bowels, I gazed spellbound at the constantly moving lights in the neighbourhood. The wind that was always blowing around the balcony. And the lights of Tokyo that I could see from the balcony were becoming more and more beautiful every year.

As I gazed at the lights, I couldn't help thinking about what would be the most appropriate kind of death for Mii. The truth was that the best would be for her to sleep in the depths of withered leaves, trees and soil, but she was unable to go anywhere any more so would have to meet her end here. Gazing at the lights, I opened the windows wide. The breeze blew through. I was happy that there was always a breeze, maybe because being high up we were surrounded by space. The breeze from the east to the north blew away the unavoidable smell emanating from Mii's body. Every time I opened the windows, it cleared the stuffiness.

If I could, I would have liked to place Mii in this cool breeze. Her body would gradually turn into dust, like in Tibetan sky burials. Since ancient times, animals had known when and how they would die. I had heard of cats choosing to die in dried leaves, or under a floor where the breeze passes. But even if Mii wanted to, she could not seek out a place to die.

As I gazed at her sleeping, the same scene kept coming into my mind. This scene was the deserted ruins of the building we lived in. The glass windows were broken, and the walls were full of cracks made by the wind and rain. Only the light and breeze passed freely through the many gaps. The scene of my cat lying there, crumbling unseen. Just as the breeze fluttered the white plastic bags and papers on the wastelands of the reclaimed land, so the white fur on Mii's belly swayed in the breeze, then blended with the light eventually to disappear. That was nature. That was natural. While this is what I imagined, I knew she could never have that sort of death.

And so, what sort of death was suitable? Was it better to hold her as she died? Or was it better for her to die quietly while her human wasn't there? This was constantly on my mind as I heard in the sound of Mii tottering slowly around the floor, in the sound of her dragging her haunches and dripping urine, 'It's over, there's no more time left.'

The Winter Break

I spent my days at the office with my colleagues, and my nights at my desk at home in Shinagawa. In the morning, I would again go straight from home to the district my office was in. How many years had I been living that life-style? The production work I had started with my colleagues was gradually taking off, but I was constantly out of breath. Even so, I could not give up my day job. As long as there was hope, I couldn't stop running around getting my ass into gear. I was often asked what was so great about doing two jobs, but I didn't really have a good answer. Writing novels was a solitary battle. All I could say was that working with my colleagues was indispensable to me.

Don't you get tired doing two jobs? 'No, not at all,' I would have liked to say, but you only had to look at me to instantly know the truth. The result of the twenty-four hours I chose for myself, not for anyone else, showed on my face, and I always had watery eyes and shadowy circles under my eyes from the fatigue of working with typography and word processors.

One day I told Mii that I'd reached my limit. I would take some time off work. I was exhausted. The New Year break was approaching, and I decided to take more time off than I usually did.

It was the end of 1996 when I took Mii on a trip for the first time ever. I had taken her to my mother's place before, but she had never been anywhere else. For many years she had been shut up in the Shinagawa apartment, only waiting for people to come home or to visit, forgetting the smells of outdoors and the feeling of the breeze on the tip of her nose. For once I wanted to show her a bright wide-open space.

After days of careful preparation, putting some convenient pocket warmers inside her carrier and enclosing it in a black cover that was supposed to be good for keeping animals calm, we left the apartment. Mii slept the whole time. The sleeping medicine the vet had given me to keep her quiet in the train had had an effect.

Sitting beside her as she peacefully slept, I simply gazed out of the window at the landscape. We were headed for a peninsula in Mie Prefecture, south of Nagoya. There was a small cottage there that I shared with my brother's family and our mother, who lived not far away in Aichi Prefecture. I had first been attracted to its beautiful rugged and uneven coast when I still lived in my childhood home. The beauty of all the bays and the light glinting on the fins of the swimming fish had long floated in and out of my mind like a faint dream. Almost thirty years had passed since then, and by a strange turn of events I had gone with my mother to look at a piece of land, and we had decided to build a small cottage. 'Oh, how lovely it is here,' my mother had exclaimed cheerfully. 'Such gentle hills and soft light.' She was now old and had lots of aches and pains, and this had been the main motivation in our decision.

The cottage was easy to get to from Aichi, where my mother and brother's family lived, and they had been using it frequently ever since, but it was more difficult for me living in Tokyo, and I had to make up my mind and make time to go.

It was the colours of the peninsula I wanted to see most. The clear bright winter light that we didn't get in Tokyo. The fresh green foliage of the urajiro ferns and ubame oaks that were unique to the area and never withered in winter, the blue of the sea and sky, and the red camellias and white narcissi that grew everywhere. And the vivid tanned skin of the people who lived there, washed by the sea breeze. All of these were inviting colours and voices for me.

I wanted to walk together with Mii in the short time we had left in a place where we could do as we pleased.

Mii was no longer in any condition to walk. She spent the whole day lying down, waiting for her human to come home from work, and when I opened the door to the apartment she would only raise her head to look at me. And she would move her mouth in a smile of greeting.

The whole apartment stank of urine and I always left one window open whatever the season. I would come home to find her sitting in urine, and our routine was to help her go to the toilet, feed her and have a bath together. When she was feeling well she would walk unsteadily around the room, but it was a forlorn way of walking with her haunches and legs always giving way.

Every morning and night, as always, I would use my hands to help her eliminate waste from her body. I no longer remembered how many years I had been doing this, and had the feeling I had been captive to the task and the stench for ever. I wanted to get away from it, even just for a short time. I wanted to be somewhere where I could breathe clean air. And this was behind my desire to go away for the winter break.

I sat back in my seat gazing at the winter landscape as if in a daze, without opening the book I'd thrown into my bag.

The rice paddies going past the train window were a dark amber, with the stubble left after the harvest forming geometric lines. There were also vegetable fields with plastic-covered greenhouses. And I saw the large gardens of farmhouses filled with yellow and purple chrysanthemums. After we changed at Nagoya on to a local train, there began to be more gentle curves and the greenery grew darker. There were always plenty of evergreen plants on the peninsula, so it never felt dreary. And when the view opened on to the winter sea, I finally felt the joy of being free and the release of tension spreading from my core throughout my body.

Thanks to the convenient pocket warmers and several layers of pee pads, Mii's carrier was nice and warm inside. Mii stayed asleep in this cosy box all the way in the train to the cottage, and only fully woke up the next morning.

I will never forget the look on her face then, her expression stiff with fear at having been brought to an unfamiliar place. But when I helped her walk to the wooden veranda and showed her the greenery right below her, then picked her up and showed her the surrounding scenery, the fear and suspicion gradually disappeared from her face.

Just as when we'd moved from Fuchu to Kokubunji, and from Kokubunji to Shinagawa, Mii started her task of checking out the new place. Tottering along and dragging her legs throughout the cottage, she smelled everything with the tip of her nose, one thing after another. The old sofa, the legs of the kitchen table, the litter box I'd prepared when we arrived (with the same litter as always), and also her toy jaguar I'd brought from Shinagawa, the cardboard box in which I'd placed an electric heated cushion, the slippers lying on the floor, and so on. Once she'd completed her inspection, she ate the newly opened can of bonito cat food, and slowly crawled into her box.

It was exactly the same thing she always did. Seeing her do this, I felt reassured and calmed down. There was nothing to be worried about. Even though it was an unfamiliar place, Mii already knew how to familiarise herself with somewhere new. I didn't know whether this was the result of a cat learning to live with her human or whether she was just resigned to it, but elderly Mii neither protested nor resisted, just went back to sleep.

I had heard that the Japanese word for cat, *neko*, had been shortened from the phrase *neruko*, or sleeping child. The older Mii got, the longer she slept. She slept endlessly. Or maybe it was because her legs were getting weak and she couldn't walk around much any more, so there was nothing else to do but sleep. I'd also heard that the word *neko* was slang for a geisha, so you had the Shinbashi *neko*, the Akasaka *neko*, the Shinagawa *neko*. This sweet, timid cat had innocently entertained me for over twenty years, with her voice, her mannerisms, her entire body . . . By now, though, my own personal charming geisha was just a bag of sleep.

When my sister finally managed to get through the busy year end at work and joined us a few days later at the cottage, Mii merely raised her face to look at her. When she was young, she would unhesitatingly go up to anyone new and sniff them. If she liked them, she would look up at their face and give a charming little *mya!* If she didn't like them, she would just ignore them.

This time, when my sister greeted her 'Mii-tan, it's me!' she did respond with a miaow, but ignored her thereafter. It seemed that Mii no longer had the energy to greet people properly. She just looked at my sister as if to say, 'You're here at last, are you?', and then curled up and went back to sleep.

I laughed, amused at how unsociable she was, like a tired old woman.

We spent the next few days in the light of the quiet peninsula. It was a private New Year's, free of the sound of traffic, just the wind in the trees. I talked on the phone with my mother, who had refused to travel in the cold weather even though we'd invited her, but I didn't get any work calls. It was a warm, peaceful way to start the new year.

With nothing else to do, my sister and I went for walks on the deserted hillside and maze of paths around the bay. We followed paths where out-of-season wild red silverberries swayed and the desiccated flowers of tall heartleaf lilies fluttered in the breeze, collecting berries and vines. My sister used these to weave wreaths and baskets, while I stitched together old mosquito nets to make a room divider decorated with woven twigs, and we adorned the windows and walls with the dried flowers of the weeds we'd picked.

Mii watched these twilight activities with a sleepy face. During the day she would drag herself into the light shining in through the windows, but when the sun went down in the afternoon she would once again crawl into her box. She had an absent, forlorn look on her face as though she didn't know where she was, or didn't even know that she wasn't in Shinagawa.

The warm days continued. After a late breakfast, my sister and I would pick Mii up and take her to the hillside outside the cottage to help her go to the toilet on the soil. She had grown used to the wooden floor in Shinagawa and I wanted her to remember the feel of earth under her paws. She had been living for nearly fifteen years in a place with no soil. This was my one regret, and I wanted her to experience it once more.

At first, she seemed to back away in a state of high alert. She was scared of this unfamiliar place. She had very possibly forgotten what soil was, its smells and sensations. This elderly cat had forgotten the wild and didn't even look up at the birds singing overhead that long ago would have made her eyes glitter. She didn't even sniff the breeze.

But maybe, I thought, after a few days of being in nature she would recover some of her sense of the wild.

My sister went back to Tokyo before me, saying she had to get back to work. In the quiet afternoon, as always I held Mii on the ground outside, put my hand under her belly searching for her round, distended bladder. I enclosed it in my palm and squeezed, and once it was empty of urine I then worked on getting the stools out, spending time on massaging her colon like a tube. Once it was all out Mii abruptly stretched her body forward as if to shake off my hand.

Until the day before, as soon as I had finished her toilet she would turn towards the cottage of her own accord as though to say she wanted to go back, but today was different. Wobbling on unsteady legs, she stretched out her head to the weeds in front of her. Could she be remembering their smell from the past? Maybe that particular weed happened to have a smell she knew.

Suddenly she bit into one of the weeds. She let go for a moment and rubbed her face against it, then took a bigger bite. And then tore off some more with her mouth. Chewing on it, she moved her body further and further along.

Mii was eating grass! And she was walking on soil! She was planting her feet firmly on the ground! She leaned her body even further into the green plants. She was engrossed in eating, choosing only young tender shoots, just as she used to do long ago. Feeling the blessings of the moment showering down on us, I supported her unsteady haunches as she continued to move further and further into the pale green urajiro ferns that were growing thickly all around.

I had thought the time she'd spent in Kokubunji had gone for ever, but here it was coming back to her in the light of the peninsula. This moment was making up for everything she had lost in the apartment floating in space in Shinagawa.

Speechless, I stood rooted to the spot in the warm light. I held my breath, wanting to listen for ever to the subtle movements of Mii's haunches, the firm movements of her jaw and grinding of teeth as she chewed on

the plants. And I could feel the winter sun on my back.
I would never forget its warmth. A vast, rich bundle of
light, a wide, infinitely absorbing light, pouring down
on us from above and reflecting from low down by the
ground, embracing the two of us.

One   I count
Two   my cat walking
Before her, green   behind her, green too
We smiled in the earth's embrace
We smiled, though our time is up

White narcissi in bloom
Thickets of sasanqua
In this town   the plop plop of flowers falling in
   the afternoon
The distant roar of the sea in full tide
Ah, the shower of time   calling
I could not chase after it
But I could listen to it

Her body opens   to the sound of winter
She won't be here next year I know
I know we won't have this time again
On this bright afternoon   overcome with an
   unfathomable sadness
The greenery shines   in my cat's gentle eyes

5

Into the Light

Summer – the Final Nights

Late at night on 25 July 1997, six months after we came home from the peninsula, my cat died. Mii spent practically all of this time lying down with bodily fluids flowing quietly out of her, and me cleaning them up until finally there were none left and she breathed her last.

I knew it was the end on 5 July. The reason I remember that day so well is that I came home from work to find Mii in a terrible state. She was lying in her box in a pool of excrement. It was as though the entire contents of her intestines had emptied out as soft, watery poop.

Her legs and belly were sopping wet. Was it something she ate? But I was sure there was nothing that was hard to digest in her food by then. She refused to eat solids, as though her body wouldn't accept them any more. If she did eat anything, it was only ever a tiny amount. So where on earth had all this excrement come from?

I picked Mii up out of this awful mess and ran with her to the bathtub, where I washed her body in warm water with the nice-smelling herbal shampoo I always used. Those days she seemed concerned about her own smell too, since normally after I washed her she buried her face in her nice-smelling fur and licked it thoroughly. But that night was different. As soon as I began washing her, she started gasping for breath, her teeth chattering.

I hastily lifted her out of the bath and dried her with a towel, but even then she didn't stop panting. Although it was summer, I got the heater out, put the towel on top of it, and waited for her breathing to settle. But from that night on, she refused to eat anything at all. She remained lying in her small box under the kitchen table, her eyes wide open. She no longer slept. Even when I got up in the middle of the night to go to the toilet, or when I woke up in the morning and went straight to check on her, her eyes were wide open and staring.

On 14 July, Mii lapped up a little water and raw egg. That was her last meal. Now that she refused all food, she became emaciated, and lay still with her legs neatly arranged, waiting patiently for something. Even when I called her name, she didn't reply. It was as though she didn't hear me, and her slightly open eyes were not seeing me but something far away. The fur all over her body stood on end, and when I stroked her over and over it just stood straight back up again. She flinched from my touch, as though her skin was sensitive from goosebumps.

I no longer turned on the light in the kitchen. I enclosed her box with more cardboard and covered it with a big sheet to prevent the light from dazzling her. There in her private room, she kept changing her position, pivoting around on her haunches like a spinning top. She was unable to stand, but she was so quiet I didn't know whether she was in pain or not. Her eyes remained open as before. She didn't eat anything, so her belly got thinner and thinner by the day. Even if I offered her some water, she didn't try to drink.

Whenever a friend called, I would whisper, 'My cat is dying. I'll call you later.'

But I couldn't take time off work, so every morning I tiptoed out of the flat, closing the door behind me, and after work I rushed straight home without stopping anywhere on the way, arriving out of breath. When I opened the door, Mii would always be in the same place, only her head slightly turned from the morning.

Every time I left home, I was sure I was going to find that Mii had died on my return. More than once or twice I'd left home with the premonition that today she would be gone for sure. But still she lived. Without eating or drinking anything . . .

I don't remember much about how I got through this time. Late at night, I couldn't bear to see Mii there with her eyes open, so I would sometimes go outside and walk round and round the area, or sit on the stairs leading down to the car park where we used to go for walks together, blown by the dawn breeze. Maybe now, in this moment, her breathing had stopped. I sometimes thought it was because I didn't want to see that happen that I kept sitting here.

Other nights I would drink alcohol and walk round and round the fence enclosing the apartment building. I told myself over and over again, Mii is dying, Mii will die any moment now. I somehow had to accept this. I had to prepare myself for the fact that my partner was going to die today or tomorrow.

For two weeks Mii lay there still alive, all skin and bones, her dishevelled fur still bristling. Finally, while I was working late at night on 25 July, she gave two or three little coughs as if calling me. It was a hard *ka-ka* sound, like something being kicked. Surprised, I went over to her and she coughed again. This time it was a quiet cough, like a whisper. The moment she died.

I picked her up, and saw her mat was stained with a small spot of blood, about the size of the tip of my little finger, the blood she had coughed up as she died. Amazingly, the place she had been lying all this time was otherwise clean. Her eyes were already closed. I put my cheek on her belly, but her heart that I had so often played at listening to had stopped.

'Mii,' I called. 'Mii!' No reply. She had always answered *mi* but now her voice was nowhere to be heard.

It was over. It was all over. Our twenty years together, the two of us . . .

I couldn't tell if the summer's night was hot or cold, but still I took out the bags of ice I had ready in the freezer, and placed them around Mii's body wrapped in a white cloth. Then I called my sister and told her,

'Mii just died.' Afterwards I simply sat motionless at her side. I don't know how much time passed, and it is possible I dozed off. Before I knew it, the pale white light of morning was shining in through the window, and as though drawn by that light, I went outside. In Mii's moment of death, I wanted to decorate her body with things she had loved.

All I could think of was weeds. Nondescript weeds growing by the road. Weeds that had been growing all over the place in Fuchu and Kokubunji. Now I saw they were growing profusely everywhere I looked. Starwort, Job's tears, wild oats. I grabbed armfuls of these weeds from the grounds of a nearby elementary school and the narrow empty plot outside a small apartment building across the street. When I got home, I arranged them around Mii's body bathed in the morning light.

There was nothing left to do. As I sat beside Mii, my tears came streaming out. Even when my father suddenly died, and when I split up with my husband, and when Tsune and Shiiko died, I hadn't cried as much as I did now. My head was so heavy with tears I couldn't lift it up.

I must have fallen asleep like that. I was woken by the doorbell. H was standing outside.

'How is your cat?'

I had been telling everyone I knew that Mii spent all her time asleep and that I thought it was the end. H had been so concerned for me she had come to ask how Mii was doing.

'I made some watermelon sherbet. I thought you might like some . . .'

I took the pale pink, refreshing-looking sherbet from her and said, my voice choking, 'My cat died last night.'

'Oh my,' H said. Shocked, she took a step back. She must have already noticed my puffy face. 'I see,' she said gently. 'I'm so sorry, I didn't know. But anyway, please eat it, and keep your spirits up.'

I slumped down beside Mii, and ate the cold sherbet. The juice from the sweet crunchy watermelon sherbet soaked into my dehydrated, strangely shaky body.

'She lived for over twenty years,' H had said to me before she left. 'She was definitely happy with you. And you were happy too, weren't you, Inaba-san?'

Yes, I was happy. I had been happy living with Mii for over twenty years, I thought as I ate the sherbet. It was so cool and refreshing, and an effective stimulant. Now all that was left to do was to say my final farewells to Mii.

Light was shining outside the window, the light of the sun just showing its face over the sea in Shinagawa. The light I had greeted so many times in the city. But today it was a different colour, utterly unlike the light I was used to. For the first time I was starting my day without hearing Mii's voice. From now on, all my mornings would be without Mii. Mornings without her nuzzling me with her head, without the smell of her body. I gazed vacantly at the light. I didn't know whether I would ever get used to this, my first taste of the light of mornings without Mii.

> *The night split   split and never closed*
> *Somewhere   an awkward crow of a chicken*
> *Gingko and azalea and robinia*
> *The plants you loved   long ago*
> *Passed overhead like shadows*
> *Before I knew it   you were   gone*
>
> *Your white belly   your back dappled yellow*
>   *and black*
> *Your life growing faint   lingering, fading,*
>   *disappearing*
> *Even as it disappears it makes a sound*
> *I was listening to, not seeing*
> *Your mouth stained with blood*
> *The sound fades   the colour fades   all is quiet*
>
> *Your time in your body receded like the tide*
>   *leaving it empty*
> *The dawn   sunrise*
> *A single unmoving point in a world on the move*
> *The newspaper came but there was nothing in it I*
>   *wanted to read*
>
> *I went to pick some flowers*
> *In the schoolyard where the chicken crowed at dawn*
> *Wanting to decorate you only in green   I pick*
>   *starwort*

Making bunches of summer weeds
I place them around my cat's head
She says nothing   a pretty ornament
For yes
She is now in another space   no longer of
  this world
My cat will never call me again

The Storm Passes

In the long past, when I was still a child, our pet cats and dogs were always buried in our back garden. Our goldfish, turtle, canary, finch – all had their graves in this garden.

My father dug the hole, and after my father died it became my mother's role. We filled it in with the black soil making a mound, placed flowers cut from the garden on top, and then placed a home-made grave marker with their name written on it. The board of wood with their name written in black letters would soon be washed clean by the wind and rain so you could no longer read the name, and the mound of earth also gradually sank down so that eventually you no longer remembered where you had buried them.

Then, with summer the weeds would come out in force, new shoots would sprout, and the grave itself would disappear. Yet whenever we stood in the garden, we would naturally remember the animals who had lived with us for a short time.

It was around here, you know, where we buried the

canary, my mother would say as she transplanted the new shoots from a pink or scattered some flower seeds she'd been given, and for us the garden was a place where old life and new life were intricately intermingled. I doubt we ever cremated any of our pets when they died. That was just how it was back then.

But living as I did in a flat in Tokyo, I had nowhere to bury my cat. Nor was there anywhere I could make a grave for her. Getting a professional to deal with her body was the only option, and so I took her to a Buddhist temple about fifteen minutes from where I lived. This temple also had a pet cemetery, which I knew about from their advertisements for a pet cremation service.

Even the cremation was ranked, with different prices for group or solo cremation. In the case of group cremation, they kept the body until they had four (I suppose they must have refrigerated them) and cremated them all at once. The problem was there was no way to distinguish which bone remnants belonged to which animal, so for anyone wanting to follow the customary funeral practice of picking up the bones and placing them in the urn, this was not the way to go.

For Mii I chose the solo cremation, the most expensive plan at 40,000 yen. This price included transport to and from home by car and the funerary urn. Instead of making a grave for her, though, I intended to take her remains to bury in a place she had loved so much, the woods of Kokubunji.

Mii went into the furnace lying in her familiar box. The same as with humans, she was placed on the platform, a switch was flipped, and the platform carried her into the furnace. By this time rigor mortis had set in and she was a little shrunken, her features already changed since last night.

With her face half buried in her blanket, she had gathered all her legs into one place as though that were the proper etiquette for animals. She had also hidden the place her excretions came from with her tail, so maybe that was the proper etiquette too. Even her death, practically from starvation, had been her own form of etiquette, so there would not be any excretions from her body when she died. A quiet body refusing to be washed or wiped any more.

That body was now being consumed by flames in the furnace. Wind and fire were passing through Mii's empty body. I could see this in my mind as I listened to the sound of the furnace.

The room next to the crematorium in the basement of the temple was the pet cemetery. The dimly lit room was lined with rows of shelves resembling bookcases, fitted with small partitions, each of which was an animal's tomb. Inside these small boxes, placed alongside photographs, mortuary tablets, flowers and incense, were plates of water and pet food, probably the animal's favourite food, maybe snacks or dried fish.

North, south, east, west. Each of the shelves had a

name prefixed with one of the cardinal directions, and they were all decorated slightly differently, with the price varying according to how auspicious its placement. Within those numerous square boxes, the souls of thousands of animals jostled for space.

And the thoughts and emotions of all the people who had lost a pet were crammed into this room too. Alongside the roar of the furnace, it was filled with the prayers of all the owners for whom it was the only way to console themselves.

The sound of the furnace gradually grew quieter. And stopped. Using the special chopsticks, I picked up Mii's still-hot bones. Her terribly thin white bones. The sound of the last ones being tipped into the funerary urn. White bones that would fit on to the palm of my hand. That having supported her flesh for twenty years, was all that was left of her.

In the car on the way home, the temple worker casually looked up at the sky and said, 'It's going to rain tonight. Seems there's a typhoon headed this way.' 'Really?' I answered. I hadn't known about the typhoon. A stilted conversation between strangers.

Consumed by flames   my cat's coffin
Her mouth demanding   I want this   I want to
*   eat that*
I want to play   still open in the flames
Her drooping tail   curled around her

176

Shrinking   turning to dust
Only her mouth open wide

We have reached the end of our journey together
I come home holding your bones
The apartment is the same as I left it
Split open   full of light

A single drop of blood on the mat
Holding my cat's bones   I kneel down
This trace of her   a sign of the end
This single drop   a sign of goodbye

Later that afternoon, I headed for Kokubunji with the white bones.

I wanted to return Mii's body to the place she loved most as soon as possible. I was never able to actually ask her where her favourite place really was. But I had the feeling that returning her to the place where her youthful, energetic body used to roam suited her best. After all these years confined to playing in our apartment floating in mid-air, if I was going to return her anywhere, then that was where it had to be.

It had started raining. Typhoon No.9 of the season was already approaching the Kanto area. I hurried from Kokubunji to Koigakubo. In the gathering dark and atrocious weather, my sneakers sopping wet, I headed for the familiar old shrine grounds.

I knew that the house we used to live in had already

been rebuilt. Just once, when work had brought me close to Kokubunji, I had walked over to see where we used to live. The old wooden house that I had loved so much had been replaced with a two-storey reinforced-concrete house. It had possibly been rebuilt right after we moved out. I could tell that some time had passed by the slight dull tinge to its white walls.

Only the concrete-block wall that the cats had walked along was still there, and lots of trees remained around the shrine.

How many years had passed since then? For a moment I stood stock-still in the rain.

The woods of the shrine by the house had been turned into a park. Almost all the cedars that had provided such pleasant green shade had been felled and replaced with grass and flower beds. The park had a slide and a sandpit and lots of azalea and forsythia bushes, but not many shaded areas. It looked bland.

This was where Mii had once roamed, and where a younger me had lived with my husband. In the back of my mind I saw my still-young husband, his thin back and long arms and legs, as he went out looking for Mii when she hadn't come home. A scene and a person lost for ever, a moment from almost twenty years ago that flitted through my mind like a distant vision.

I stood there in the park clutching Mii's white bones in my hand as the rain intensified and the wind began to pick up. The landscape had changed, but there was no doubting that this was Mii's place. Alongside the concrete-block wall there were weeds and bushes and the smell of soil. Beyond the wall where Mii had often walked, there was also a field of azalea belonging to a landscape gardening business, unchanged from the past.

I buried the small fragments of white bone here and there along the route where Mii had once roamed. I buried lots and lots so that she could follow them back to the place she had loved. The sensation of the soft, sticky earth. Oh, this earth! The black clayey soil that stuck to your feet as you walked. Filling my lungs with the smell of this earth, I walked on, burying Mii's bones.

After the typhoon had passed, it would be followed by beautiful clear weather. Once the storm was over and the sky had brightened, you would be able to follow this path to your old haunts.

There was a sandpit, and plenty of undergrowth. Maybe you'd meet up with the souls of the stray cats you knew long ago. The black and white cat you once loved must be there too. And the single foetus you carried briefly in your womb. And this path would lead you to a place where you would smell the robinia flowers.

Now that I thought of it, you had reached the age of twenty. I wanted to see you off as I would my child leaving home upon reaching the age of maturity.

Buffeted by the wind and pelted by the rain, I thought of all the cats long ago, rolling around on the ground after the rain had stopped. A smile came to my lips.

'Souls circle in the rays of light . . .' A beautiful phrase I'd read somewhere. Or maybe it was, 'God is in the light'?

It was true, spirits and departed souls circled in the light that came streaming down. I didn't have any particular faith, but the one thing I did believe in was light. Just being in warm light, I could be with the people and the cat I had lost from my life.

My mornings without Mii would start tomorrow. But this was a new time for me. I might weep, but I wouldn't mourn. Mii had returned to the light, and I would still be able to meet her there hundreds, thousands of times again.

Two days later, in the afternoon, the thick cloud cover finally broke and the light shone through. In a moment, the summer light spread across the sky and, unusually for central Tokyo, I was enveloped in a distinct fragrance of trees.

The Leopard

The leopard is one of Harvill's historic colophons and an imprimatur of the highest quality literature from around the world.

When The Harvill Press was founded in 1946 by former Foreign Office colleagues Manya Harari and Marjorie Villiers (hence Har-vill), it was with the express intention of rebuilding cultural bridges after the Second World War. As their first catalogue set out: 'The editors believe that by producing translations of important books they are helping to overcome the barriers, which at present are still big, to close interchange of ideas between people who are divided by frontiers.' The press went on to publish from many different languages, with highlights including Giuseppe Tomasi di Lampedusa's *The Leopard*, Boris Pasternak's *Doctor Zhivago*, José Saramago's *Blindness*, W. G. Sebald's *The Rings of Saturn*, Henning Mankell's *Faceless Killers* and Haruki Murakami's *Norwegian Wood*.

In 2005 The Harvill Press joined with Secker & Warburg, a publisher with its own illustrious history of publishing international writers. In 2020, Harvill Secker reintroduced the leopard to launch a new translated series celebrating some of the finest and most exciting voices of the twenty-first century.

Jonas Hassen Khemiri: *The Family Clause*
    trans. Alice Menzies
Karl Ove Knausgaard: *In the Land of the Cyclops: Essays*
    trans. Martin Aitken
Karl Ove Knausgaard: *The Morning Star*
    trans. Martin Aitken
Karl Ove Knausgaard: *The Wolves of Eternity*
    trans. Martin Aitken
Karl Ove Knausgaard: *The Third Realm*
    trans. Martin Aitken
Antoine Leiris: *Life, After*
    trans. Sam Taylor
Édouard Louis: *A Woman's Battles and Transformations*
    trans. Tash Aw
Édouard Louis: *Change: A Method*
    trans. John Lambert
Geert Mak: *The Dream of Europe: Travels in the Twenty-First Century*
    trans. Liz Waters
Layla Martínez: *Woodworm*
    trans. Sophie Hughes & Annie McDermott
Haruki Murakami: *First Person Singular: Stories*
    trans. Philip Gabriel
Haruki Murakami: *Murakami T: The T-Shirts I Love*
    trans. Philip Gabriel
Haruki Murakami: *Novelist as a Vocation*
    trans. Philip Gabriel & Ted Goossen

Ngũgĩ wa Thiong'o: *The Perfect Nine: The Epic of Gĩkũyũ and Mũmbi*
trans. the author
Kristín Ómarsdóttir: *Swanfolk*
trans. Vala Thorodds
Intan Paramaditha: *The Wandering*
trans. Stephen J. Epstein
Per Petterson: *Men in My Situation*
trans. Ingvild Burkey
Andrey Platonov: *Chevengur*
trans. Robert Chandler & Elizabeth Chandler
Mohamed Mbougar Sarr: *The Most Secret Memory of Men*
trans. Lara Vergnaud
Dima Wannous: *The Frightened Ones*
trans. Elisabeth Jaquette
Emi Yagi: *Diary of a Void*
trans. David Boyd & Lucy North